THE REMARKABLE
ORPHAN KID'S R   ᴜᴄᴄᴇss

Smelly Kid

ANDY LEE
WITH Dave Taylor

Copyright © Andy Lee & Dave Taylor 2025

The moral right of this author has been asserted.

All rights reserved.

No part of this publication may be reproduced, stored in a retrieval system, or transmitted, in any form or by any means, without the prior permission in writing of the publisher, nor be otherwise circulated in any form of binding or cover other than that in which it is published and without a similar condition including this condition being imposed on the subsequent purchaser.

Editing, design, typesetting and publishing by UK Book Publishing

www.ukbookpublishing.com

ISBN: 978-1-917329-56-9

Smelly Kid

Prelude

The gentle stroking of my hair stirred me from sleep. "You need to be strong now, Andy," John's voice whispered. "Be a big boy for your brothers and sister."

I was 12 years old, and felt so confused. It was around seven in the morning. I couldn't understand why John was in my bedroom, stroking my head. For 11 years, I had called him Dad. John was Dad, though not the kind of father other boys had.

He wasn't in a relationship with Mum and had rarely ever lived at home. John had never tucked me in, played games, or bought me a single toy. Yet, I had always understood that he was Dad to me and two of my siblings, Patrick and Aoife.

But that all changed one day when I was out walking with Mum and Aunty Linda.

"Andy, you know your dad John?" Mum asked. "Well, he isn't your real dad. He is Patrick and Aoife's dad, but not yours. Your birth father was an English man I met on the Isle of Man when I was 18. His name was Jason. He was a mechanic, and I have no idea where he is now."

SMELLY KID

It was like my world had flipped upside down as I tried to process what Mum was telling me.

I had a dad called John, a terrible dad who did nothing parental, but at least I knew who he was. Now, my dad was a man I'd never met, and nobody knew anything about him. This seemed a recurring theme in my life: one day I had something, the next day I didn't.

Why was John in my room, stroking my hair? Where was Mum? No one told me. I felt uneasy as I was instructed to get up and dressed. I likely stank of piss from wetting the bed, but no one said anything as I did it every single night and nobody seemed to care any more.

Downstairs, there were more people in my house, and they were all crying. Sherrie, who had been babysitting us, was still there, crying. My mum's friend Martina was crying too. They all looked at me with sad expressions; the silence felt eerie.

No one told me what was going on.

John said we were going to his apartment on the other side of the city. Without a car or money for a taxi, we had to take our bikes. It was a cold September morning, and I had my little brother Patrick sitting on the crossbar, and John had Aoife. It took ages as I was just a little, tired kid, pedalling as fast as I could, chilled to the bone.

PRELUDE

We arrived at John's apartment, and I made my brother and sister some hot tea. The only food was bread, no butter or jam. But that was okay. Dry bread was more than I got a lot of mornings.

John was still acting strangely. I felt like he had something to tell us. Some deeper sense gave me a feeling that I didn't want to hear whatever it was he was struggling to say. So I never said anything. It was oddly quiet. I remember the silence as it was unusual. I was used to noise. All of the time. Living with five younger brothers and a sister meant that chaos and noise was normal.

Eventually, John sat us all down and casually said, "Your mum was out last night at a party. There was a car crash and she died."

The words felt like a punch hard in my stomach. The feeling of pain was overwhelming and I felt like I was gonna be sick. My young brain struggled to understand.

Mum was all I had. I didn't have any toys, my only pair of shoes had a hole in the sole and the air bubble was sticking out the side. I had no real friends because we kept on moving schools. I thought I had a dad until that was taken away, and now I was being told I no longer had Mum. She had been my whole world, and in just one sentence, she was gone.

Patrick and Aoife were eerily silent. They were too young to comprehend what was being said.

SMELLY KID

Amidst the confusion and anguish, John left us to go to the pub. We were suddenly alone in his strange apartment, with no adults to care for us. I kept thinking it wasn't real, and Mum would come and get us. Then, I heard her name on the radio as the news reported the crash that had killed her. A drunk driver had been arrested. Mum was never coming to get me, and from that moment, my life was forever changed.

I realise, dear reader, if you came here expecting raunchy tales about "Andy Lee, Ireland's most famous porn star", the well-endowed cheeky chap, who entertains with his raunchy content, then that opening might have been a bit of a shock! Apologies about that.

Don't worry, I'll be getting to all that fun stuff later, but first, let's uncover the story behind Andy Lee's rise to fame. To do that, we need to go right back to the very beginning. I'm Andy Lee and this is my story.

Chapter One

"SMELLY KID"

My earliest memory is of Mum handing Patrick and me a little paper bag at Christmas, telling us that Santa had brought us gifts. I was so excited and tore open my bag to discover some little plastic dinosaurs. As I got older and our family grew, Santa's visits became less frequent.

There were lots of kids at home. I remember Mum nearly always being pregnant. I was the oldest, then there was Patrick and Aoife. Next up was Dan, followed by Connor, and finally Ryan who was only a baby when Mum was killed.

My first home that I remember was Dorset Street Flats, in the middle of Dublin's North Inner City. It was a notorious place in Ireland when I was a kid. Its old buildings and stone streets showed a long history, but there was a darker side to the neighbourhood. In the 1990s, when I lived there, the area was consumed by a heroin epidemic. It was often scary, and the sound of police cars was always around. Even though things were tough, the people there were strong and helped each other out where possible.

I was always outside, playing with the neighbourhood kids, making our own toys out of bits of scrap that was lying around. Everyone was poor. I remember Mum had a job at the local corner shop for a while, but that stopped as more siblings appeared. No job and more hungry mouths meant less food for me. It wasn't unusual for me to be told to ask next door if we could 'borrow' a few slices of bread or a cup of milk. The sheer embarrassment of having to ask still stings. Sometimes there were days where there was no food for us older kids to eat at home at all. Not a scrap. I would try to sleep with an empty tummy, my stomach growling.

Not knowing any different, I didn't realise just how poor we were growing up. It's hard to miss what you've never had. I remember a time when I visited a friend's house and saw their fridge filled with food. I was amazed and a little envious. It was then that I realised our circumstances were not normal for every kid. Being invited to other people's homes happened less. I now know why. I was always filthy. My unwashed hair, riddled with nits. I could barely hold a knife and fork. Of course nobody wanted me in their house. In an environment where everyone around me was poor, our family stood out as having a significantly higher level of deprivation.

CHAPTER ONE

Cholaiste Mhuire, an all-boys Catholic school just across the road from Dorset Street Flats, was where I attended school. It was a Gaelscoil, part of a growing movement in Ireland during the 1990s to revive the Irish language. The goal was to immerse students in a Gaelic-speaking environment, meaning all subjects were taught exclusively in Irish. Again, I didn't know any other way of learning so it just felt normal to me.

Most of the kids at school were poor, so in some ways, I didn't stand out being a scruffy, often nit-ridden kid. Though some of the boys seemed to have it slightly easier than me. I was jealous of the food they brought in for lunch. Some kids would have a plastic lunch box, with a proper sandwich filled with some delicious meat or cheese. Plus they would have a packet of crisps, biscuits, a piece of fruit, and a bottle of juice. A really good day for me would be a few slices of bread and jam, maybe with a dollop of butter, and a juicy apple. Sadly there were lots of bad days where I had nothing at all. The smell of the other kids' lunches would fill the air, making my stomach rumble even louder.

My mum did her best, but it was tough to make ends meet, and it's hard to say this now, but often her best just wasn't good enough.

Every Wednesday, we had PE lessons, and I would struggle to fit in, as I never had the proper gym shoes or tracksuit. It was a constant battle to keep up with the other kids and not feel like the odd boy out. I tried to hide my embarrassment, but I knew I was different from the other kids.

One bright spot in my school life was a teacher, Mr Brian O'Toole. He seemed to have a genuine connection with my mum and always looked out for me. Sometimes, he would go above and beyond, sending food to our home or giving me a small gift at Christmas. His warm smile and kind words always made me feel a bit better. His kindness and support were a great comfort during those difficult times.

But even with Brian looking out for me, I struggled with lessons. I couldn't concentrate and struggled to keep up with even basic reading and writing. So apologies, dear readers, if this book isn't filled with big, fancy words.

I felt stupid and ashamed, knowing that I was falling behind my classmates. I was also so embarrassed about my handwriting and dreaded being asked to write stuff down. I still am. Mr O'Toole would often pull me aside and say, "Don't worry, Andy, everyone learns at their own pace." His words were always a source of encouragement, even though I knew he was just trying to make me feel better.

Looking back, I think part of the problem is that I was always tired. I'd sit at my desk, struggling to stay awake. At home, there were barely any bedtime

CHAPTER ONE

rules or routine. I played outside till I was tired and then went to sleep. But I always wet the bed. Every single night. I hated it. The cold, damp sheets against my skin made me shiver. There was so much shame, and it always woke me up.

Mum would sometimes try and help. There wasn't always clean sheets, so she would put a towel over the wet patch but it barely kept me dry. I eventually stopped telling Mum in the end. Instead, if I woke up and the bed was wet, I'd hop in with my brother or sister, but then I might wet their bed too. I felt like a burden. Mum did try and get me help. I went to different doctors, and tried various treatments, including bed wetting alarms, but I was so tired I slept through it. Unfortunately nobody found a solution. Interestingly, however, I never wet the bed again from the day my mum died.

So part of my problem at school was that I was always exhausted. I'm also certain I have ADHD. There will be more about that later, but I just struggled with concentrating on anything. Often, I just didn't go to school and stayed out playing. Mum didn't really care that much, so neither did I.

I slipped so far behind with elementary teachings, I got kept behind a year at school. I ended up in the same class as my little brother Patrick – this just meant further shame and humiliation.

SMELLY KID

Brian was like my guardian angel. There was one time he came to our house in the middle of winter and discovered Mum had us all huddled in the kitchen, with one gas ring burning on the stove. The only heat we had in the entire home. I don't know how he managed it, but he then made sure Mum had the means to heat the house for a while. There was one highlight of my childhood that I am indebted to Brian for arranging: my trips to Sunshine House.

Chapter Two

"SUNSHINE HOUSE"

One of the highlights of my early childhood was going to Sunshine House: a week of pure fun in the seaside town of Balbriggan.

This was a charity, run by volunteers specifically aimed at disadvantaged kids. Every year, all the deprived kids from around my area would be added to a list and names would be drawn at random. I'm not sure exactly how it all worked, but being chosen was like winning the golden ticket!

We would go by train and that was a thrill in itself. We would depart from Tara Street train station, in the business district of south Dublin's inner city. This was a huge old imposing building that was filled with posh people going about their business in smart suits and shiny shoes, clutching their briefcases. Us scruffy kids must have looked so out of place, but I thought it was all such a great adventure. As the parents said goodbye, the friendly team from Sunshine House were there to greet us,

SMELLY KID

with big smiles and open arms. I'd be looking at their faces, hoping to see my favourite volunteers that I'd met the previous year.

The train driver would toot the horn as the train departed and rattled along the tracks. We'd be waving goodbye to our family with mixed emotions, super excited about what lay ahead, but also worried about leaving everyone behind. Some of us would be trying hard not to cry in front of the other kids. The train was like a big iron beast, chugging its way towards adventure. As I looked out the window, the fields and hills were a blur of green, a lovely sight after being cooped up in the city. The volunteers would be entertaining us, playing games and leading us in sing songs.

Sunshine House was a big, old building – it felt to me like a castle or something. We were split into groups, each with a saint's name, boys and girls separated and sent off to our dorms. These were kids from all over Ireland that I didn't know and it was so good for me to have that freedom from being known as the stinky, dumb kid. I was so excited to escape my everyday life and have a great time.

We spent hours running free. Playing on the beach, splashing in the waves and laughing and joking the whole time. The feeling of the warm sand between my toes made the experience even more magical.

CHAPTER TWO

Every day was packed with adventures. We'd build sandcastles and participate in hole digging competitions. It was the best fun. The noise of us kids screaming and giggling sticks with me today.

In the afternoon, we'd go on hunts for Ice Pops, hidden all over the place. Finding a tasty, cold Ice Pop was like finding a pot of gold at the end of a rainbow.

Evenings were a blast. We'd watch cartoons and dance like madmen under the disco lights. It was a chance to let our hair down and have a bit of craic.

One of my favourite memories of my stay at Sunshine House was when the leaders told us the spooky story about Mr Mackenzie's ghost. We were all huddled together, trembling with a mix of excitement and fear. All the kids were holding hands, too scared to let go. We all squeezed tighter as the storyteller described the ghost's haunting presence. It was both thrilling and terrifying, but it's a memory I'll cherish forever.

The story told of how Mackenzie's ghost would wander the corridors at night, his mournful presence felt by those who dared to venture alone. It was said that he was particularly drawn to the toilets, where his tragic end had occurred. Looking back as an adult, I realise that the ghost story might have been a clever tactic by the organisers to deter us from running to the toilets all night long. But regardless of the reason, it was a fun and spooky tale that got our imagination running wild and brought us all closer together.

It was meant to be a lottery that selected the kids for Sunshine House; however, my name always seemed to be chosen. Sometimes I'd even get to go twice a year. Once again it was teacher Brian to the rescue. He knew how deprived my family was and how important that week of care and respite was to us kids. It wasn't just us little ones that got a break, I'm sure Mum also welcomed the downtime whilst we were away to have fewer kids to look after. So Brian fought for us to go there. He broke all the rules. Even taking us down himself in his little car. I understand now that Brian was the stable male figure in my life that I desperately needed and likely craved. Brian often would walk us kids down from Sunshine House to the beach and I'd latch on to him, putting my tiny little hand in his. Feeling safe and protected.

The Sunshine House was more than just a camp; it was a summer week of pure joy. It was a place where I could be myself, make new mates, and have a ball. What made it extra special for me was that they made sure us kids were equal. We all had £5 spending money. Nobody was allowed more. We were even given matching sets of pyjamas. For once I didn't stand out. I still wet the bed but I just remember being treated so kindly. I'd usually wake up first because my bed was damp and the leaders would send me to shower whilst they changed my bed for me. That meant I could hop back into a dry bed and when the other boys woke up they were none the wiser.

When I returned home I'd be so keen to tell Mum all about my adventures and show her a toy I'd been given and I'd often return with a set of new clothes. The memories I made there are like a treasure chest, full of laughter and good times.

Chapter Three

"THE NIGHT THE MOB CAME"

It was the mid-1990s, and Dublin was gripped by a heroin epidemic that cast a dark shadow over once-vibrant neighbourhoods. Overdoses and crime rates soared, leaving a sense of fear and despair in the community.

In the heart of this crisis, a movement was born: Concerned Parents, a group of determined individuals, mostly mothers, united against the plague of heroin that threatened their families. Their actions, though controversial, were driven by a desperate desire to protect their children and restore a sense of safety to their communities. As a boy, I'd often accompany my mother on Concerned Parents' protest marches, their chants echoing through the streets. While I didn't fully understand the gravity of the situation, I remember the exhilarating sense of community and purpose.

We'd be chanting, "What do we want? Pushers out! When do we want it? Now! Pushers, pushers,

CHAPTER THREE

pushers, out, out, out!" We'd be carrying huge banners and homemade signs, all saying, 'Pushers Out', with images of syringes on them. These were huge, powerful gatherings. You don't mess with a determined Irish Mammy.

Speaking of which, my mother had a liking for "bad boys", and Glen fitted that mould perfectly. Glen was a charismatic guy with a rebellious charm that my mother found irresistible. He's the father of my younger brothers, Dan and Connor. My aunt later confided that she believed my mother was truly in love with him.

However, there was a dark side to Glen. He was involved with heroin, both as a user and small-time street dealer. His addiction had a profound impact on our lives, rippling through our entire family.

One evening, as we were all at home in Dorset Street Flats, amidst the usual chaos of unruly kids, a loud noise startled us. Looking out the window, we saw a massive crowd gathered outside, their faces filled with anger. They were chanting, "What do we want? Pushers out! When do we want it? Now! Pushers, pushers, pushers, out, out, out!"

It suddenly dawned on me that we had become the enemy because of Glen, who was now a part of our family. He urged us not to answer the door. But the mob was relentless, banging on our door and windows with increasing ferocity. A man with a furious face, his mouth frothing with rage, peered through my window, shouting threats and insults.

Fear gripped us all, our bodies trembling and our hearts pounding. My mother, her face pale with terror, tried desperately to protect us from the chaos, but the baying mob forced their way into our home, dragging us out onto the street. As we were pushed through the crowd, people hurled abuse and threw objects at us. My mother was sobbing, her arms wrapped tightly around us.

We were forced to walk through the angry mob, our lives in danger. The crowd followed us, shouting and threatening us. All us kids were screaming and crying, utterly terrified. We managed to escape the mob but we were not allowed to return to our home. My mother later managed to retrieve some of our belongings, but I never went back to that place. I had lost the only home I'd ever known.

That night, we sought safety at John's apartment (at that point, I still believed he was my father). Glen went his own way, returning to his parents' home. We stayed with John for a few nights before moving to a women's refuge called the Regina Ceoli. The refuge was formally a workhouse and was run by the Legion of Mary. It provided a safe haven for women and children, offering shelter, counselling, and job training.

CHAPTER THREE

Brian heard about us getting evicted and raced to Dorset Street Flats, arriving not long after the event but too late to stop it. Dan's pram was still outside. Brian was livid, hearing what the community had done to our family. Even more furious that they hadn't even allowed Mum to take the pram, as Dan was just a newborn baby. He wanted to know where we had escaped to, but nobody knew. Even worse, nobody cared. It was the dead of winter, and the icy wind was blowing a gale. Brian was fearful for our fate. He walked the streets for a few nights trying to locate us and eventually tracked us down to the refuge as he spotted our school jumpers, soaking wet, hanging on some washing lines.

Everything was very strict at Regina Ceoli. Many of the residents were addicts, others suffering with severe mental health issues. It was not a great environment for children. The mothers barely got to leave for any kind of break as they were expected to remain there to watch their children.

When Brian found us, he told Mum that us kids needed to get straight back to school. I think Mum had felt we wouldn't be welcome due to the drugs shame, but Brian was having none of that. He could see how stressed Mum was and knew that us being at school would give her space to sort herself out and make plans.

SMELLY KID

Brian helped in other ways too. Mum was barely allowed to bring any possessions, only what she could carry to the refuge in a few black bags. We had an entire flat full of our furniture and belongings, most of which ended up at Brian's house, as he was kind enough to store it for us.

Men weren't allowed in the hostel – even Brian, a Saint Vincent de Paul volunteer, initially struggled to get in as the nuns cracked the door open slightly and interrogated him! Eventually, he was allowed in the office only, where we would all go and meet him and spend time together. I know his presence and care were a great comfort to Mum.

He played a huge part in making sure we had some sort of Christmas at Regina Ceoli, providing decorations and some gifts. Brian was always in the background just doing what he could to help our family, which was in dire circumstances. As I'm writing this, I'm struggling to find adequate words to describe how grateful I am. So I'll simply say this: "Thank you, Brian."

Unfortunately, Glen even managed to ruin our stay at the Regina Ceoli. Encouraged by Mum (who was missing her "piece of rough"), he tried to sneak into the refuge but fell off the wall, cutting himself on the barbed wire, leaving him badly cut and injured. I'm not sure if the defences were to keep intruders out or the residents in. I remember the sight of blood

CHAPTER THREE

everywhere, and it led to us being kicked out from the refuge.

Being evicted from Dorset Street Flats was devastating for me. I lost everything I knew: my home, my stability, and my few possessions. I was just eight years old. One day, I had a home; the next day, I didn't. This recurring theme in my life marked the beginning of a serious decline. At that moment, I hated Glen and was angry with Mum for being involved with him.

Chapter Four

A FIGHT FOR SURVIVAL

—

Immediately after being evicted from the refuge centre, Mum took us to stay at John's place. Glen was still around, though, which triggered John, setting him off into a fit of uncontrollable rage, beating Mum badly. As his fists rained down, I can remember feeling utterly powerless as I listened to Mum being hit, punch after punch, wishing so desperately to rescue her. I'll never forget her screams of terror, begging him to stop as he spat in her face, calling her a whore. A big towering man being tough against a tiny, fragile woman.

The violence was so severe, her face black and blue, almost unrecognisable to us kids, that Mum decided to take us all to stay with her sister, my Aunt Teresa.

Life at my aunt and uncle's home was a stark contrast to what I was used to. There was a sense of routine and structure, and, most importantly, there was food! Every morning, I'd be sent off to

CHAPTER FOUR

school with a belly full of toast, cereal, and hot tea. My lunchbox was always packed with proper sandwiches. In the evenings, we would all sit down together at the table to enjoy a hot dinner, traditional Irish dinners, cooked at home.

I was also made to have regular hot baths. Patrick and I would splash around together, trying to create as many bubbles as possible. I remember they came from a blue sailor-shaped bottle of 'Mr Matey' bubble bath, and I thought it was such fun! I loved that stuff and it made bath time a proper adventure.

Teresa has later recalled that I was unusually quiet during this time. I wasn't my usual boisterous self. Looking back, I can only imagine that I was still traumatised by the upheaval of being evicted from Dorset Street Flats and the shame of being from the family that was now labelled as part of Dublin's 'drug problem', never mind seeing my mum being beaten and abused by John.

All my life, I had lived with the stigma of coming from Dorset Street Flats. People from other parts of Dublin looked down on everyone who lived there. Us Dorset Street Flats residents coped with this by forming a tight-knit community. But now, those people, my people, who had felt like my extended family, had turned on us and were treating us as 'filth'. There was no longer any 'safe space' for me to escape to.

After about three happy weeks of living with my aunt and uncle, Mum discovered she was pregnant with her fifth child, Connor. Glen was the father.

Despite everyone advising her against it, Mum wanted to be back living with Glen. She managed to secure a social home in a town called Ballybough. Once again, we were uprooted and moved on.

Ballybough was to become our home for the next four years.

Initially, the council placed us in a cottage in Croke Villas. The name 'villas' might sound exotic, but the reality was that it was another rough housing estate. We didn't stay there for long and were moved again, just five minutes away to Annesley Avenue.

Mum tried to keep us in the same school, but the problem was that we were no longer local and had to take the bus every day. We didn't mind too much, though, as our reputation for being 'scum' had preceded us, and the local kids already hated us. Avoiding school with them was a relief.

Mum would give Patrick and me £2 each day to cover our bus fare and buy lunch. The bus cost 40 pence and most days, unbeknown to Mum, we would walk nearly an hour to school and back, using the bus fare to buy extra snacks like crisps or chocolate.

Doing this long journey to try and keep us in our original school went on for a while, but Mum was struggling more and more to make ends meet. Often,

CHAPTER FOUR

she didn't have any money for us to get to school, let alone buy lunch. Eventually, the decision was made for us to change schools to somewhere closer.

Brian came to check in on us all at our new home and discovered Mum had me sitting on the fridge, attempting to cut my hair. Brian would have seen the shocking results of Mum's previous attempts to cut our hair and, once again, came to my rescue.

'Am I doing it right?' Mum asked Brian.

'Well, there is a certain knack to it. I'm not very good at it, but I'll have a go if you want,' Brian replied.

Mum promptly handed Brian the scissors and he proceeded to give me the best haircut I'd ever had. Just in time for my new school.

It was called St Josephs and I absolutely hated it. This school had kids from a wide range of social backgrounds, from the poorest to the reasonably well-off. This meant that the scruffy, smelly, poor kids really stood out. Not only that, but we were also labelled as the 'junkie family'. Additionally, in my previous school, I had only spoken in Gaelic. Now everything was taught in English, and I was so far behind academically that I had no chance of fitting in.

Kids can be cruel, and I was bullied from the beginning. I could just about handle the physical abuse. Getting kicked and punched didn't bother me too much. Bruises would always heal. It was the name-calling that really hurt. They say, "sticks and stones may break your bones, but words will never hurt you". Well, I can tell you that's not true when you're nine years old and being called 'scum', or 'smelly', or 'scroungers', and every combination of those words imaginable. I was bullied every single day. Even by some teachers. It felt like everyone hated me before they even knew me. If I dared to fight back, which I often did, I would be the one who got into trouble, not the kid who had thrown a rock at me or drenched me with a bottle of piss.

Mum tried hard to comfort me, but there was little she could do to make things better. My baby brother Connor needed looking after, and the younger kids were always a priority, which I can understand now in retrospect.

Glen was still around, but I don't really remember him living permanently with us. When he did turn up, it was always chaos.

I remember one time he barged into our house, grabbed me, and shoved a load of stolen CDs down my trousers. The police, or Garda as we called them in Ireland, were seconds behind him. I was told to keep quiet. I remember feeling sheer terror as the authorities searched our home for the contraband, while I stood trembling awkwardly in the kitchen. The police didn't hold back in expressing their opinion of us. 'Dirty thieving bastards' was a phrase they used repeatedly.

CHAPTER FOUR

Glen eventually got sent to prison for a while. I don't remember what for. It could have been anything as he was a proper 'wrong 'un'.

By this time, Mum had her second child with Glen, baby Connor. Financially, things were so tough at home that Mum couldn't feed another mouth. She was also quite sick after giving birth, with Hepatitis B, likely contracted from junkie Glen, and struggled to even wash the baby. Initially, Mum's older sister, who couldn't have kids of her own, offered to take Connor in. Mum reluctantly agreed to this. She knew it would be better for everyone as she was clearly struggling and couldn't adequately feed or clothe the family she already had. Connor was 'adopted' for only a few weeks, and then, without warning, suddenly returned, abandoned outside our local pub. Apparently, my aunt had underestimated how tough being a parent was. Social services intervened, and it was mutually agreed that Connor would be fostered.

It was an open situation and was only meant to be temporary, so Connor was still part of our family, even though he mainly lived with his foster parents. We got to see him at weekends and some holidays. After Mum passed, Connor was fully adopted by his foster family, Ann and Tony.

One time, Glen turned up unannounced at our house. He had been released from prison and was with his latest girlfriend.

I left them in the kitchen and continued watching TV in the living room.

After a while, I noticed it was quiet and discovered them both slumped on the floor, unconscious with needles in their arms.

I was so numb to this kind of thing that I just went back to watching TV, pretending nothing had happened. Eventually the pair came round from their drug induced coma, and before leaving, they robbed us. Not that there was much to take but Glen found a bit of cash Mum had stashed away and also took her mobile phone. I remember this clearly as I had to try and explain to Mum what had happened and who had taken her phone.

I also remember the days afterwards as we just had nothing at home to eat. It was really desperate times. Mum had no phone to get help and no money to travel anywhere to beg relatives for help.

It was around the age of ten that Mum told me that John wasn't my dad. This was a devastating blow. It's difficult to explain why, as John had never played any meaningful role in my life. Not as a dad, anyway. So I wasn't mourning the loss of a father so much. I think it was more the feeling of being deceived and discovering that something important I thought was true, was actually a lie.

I also grieved the absence of my real father, whom I believed was called Jason. He might as well have

CHAPTER FOUR

been dead for all I knew. But in my imagination, he was a heroic figure who, if only he found me, would rescue me from my life. I desperately craved a father figure who could protect me, and my mind painted Jason as that person.

Unfortunately, Jason never turned up, and nobody rescued me.

Mum then met another guy, Edward, who she fell for. She soon got pregnant with her sixth child, bringing my last brother, Ryan, into the home. But Edward also developed a heroin addiction and was swiftly kicked out by Mum.

School, even though it was tough, provided a sense of stability. By this time, I had learned to stand up for myself better and ignore the bullies' taunts. I even had a few friends and we all looked out for each other.

My Aunty Linda, another of my mum's sisters, lived close to us and began getting more involved in our lives, supporting Mum where she could. This meant there were fewer days where we had nothing to eat and more days where we had clean clothes to wear.

We also had a babysitter, Sherrie, who helped look after the younger ones, which took a lot of pressure off both Mum and myself. This gave me more of a chance to be a kid.

SMELLY KID

With Aunty Linda's help and Sherrie's support, I felt safer, loved, and had a chance to enjoy being a kid. So life was definitely improving. I even got to go on holiday! Mum took me to Butlin's!

***

Chapter Five

BUTLIN'S

—

The train chugged along, the wheels screaming as we got closer to Mosney. I couldn't wait to get to Butlin's! It was going to be the best week ever, especially since it was just Mum and me. With four brothers and a sister at home, one-on-one time was rare.

I couldn't believe how Mum had managed to scrimp enough money for the holiday. I don't know how she did it, but she must have saved really hard and I was so grateful to her for taking me. A couple of her friends and their kids joined us too.

Walking from the train station, we passed by the edge of the vast holiday camp and saw these huge swans on a boating lake. They were pedal boats and I couldn't wait to have a go.

We arrived at the main entrance, walked past all the flags, and were greeted by a cheery Butlin's Redcoat who showed us where to check in. The reception hall was massive! There was a huge queue of people waiting to get their chalet keys. Even though we had to wait, it was exciting. I was buzzed to find out where we were going to stay.

We finally reached the desk and got our key. The nice lady who dealt with us handed me the entertainment brochure. It was full of pictures of kids having fun in the swimming pool, playing games, and watching shows. I knew I was going to have a great time.

We headed to our little chalet, which was small but cosy, with just two single beds and a small bathroom. But we didn't stay in the chalet for long; we really only slept there. We left our suitcase and headed straight to the pool. The indoor swimming pool was massive! It had windows all down one side, so from the outside you could look in and see people swimming. It was amazing. I remember these huge mushroom-shaped fountains that towered out of the pool, with water cascading down the edges. The water was freezing at first, but it was great fun. We spent hours splashing around and going down the slides. Mum even joined in, and we had a great laugh.

After that, we hit the funfair. The rollercoaster was the best! It was so fast and scary, but it was a blast. We also went on the dodgems and the Mexican hat ride. Mum wasn't too bad at the dodgems; and kept on banging into everyone.

CHAPTER FIVE

The great thing about Butlin's was that nearly everything was included in the price, even the food. We got to eat in this huge restaurant three times a day. I don't think I'd ever eaten so much in my whole life. For some reason, I remember big metal teapots on the tables, providing endless cups of steaming hot tea.

They had a few little shops, and on the first day, I found this place that made cool little bracelets with metal tags for engraving your name. They cost £3 each, and I wanted one so badly. It was the only thing I asked for, and Mum promised me that if I was good, we could get one before I went home.

In the evenings, we went to the bingo hall or watched the Redcoats. They were hilarious, always cracking jokes and doing silly dances. But the best part was just sitting with Mum, chatting and laughing. It was so nice to have her all to myself.

We had been there for four nights when everything changed. Mum woke me up panicking, asking if I'd seen her purse. I was really groggy and couldn't quite understand what she was saying. We didn't have much stuff with us, but Mum was turning the room upside down. It turned out that someone had broken into our chalet while we were asleep and stolen her purse and watch. Mum was utterly heartbroken. With no money at all, we had no choice but to cut our holiday short and go home that day.

SMELLY KID

I was absolutely devastated. It just felt so unfair. I didn't blame Mum; she was as upset as I was. I can still remember her saying to her friends, "What have I ever done to deserve this?"

A train was leaving late that morning, and we were in a rush to pack. I couldn't stop thinking about the bracelet. Amidst the chaos, I quietly said to Mum, "I've been good, haven't I?"

"Of course you have, Andy. This isn't your fault. Why are you asking?"

"It's okay, Mum. I know I'm not going to get the bracelet."

I could see fire in her big bright blue eyes. "Yes, you are, son!" she said defiantly.

Mum dragged me and our packed suitcase to the shop. I could tell she was on a mission.

"You're going to make me a bracelet with 'Andy' written on it for my little boy, and I'm not paying for it because your camp's shitty door locks allowed some thieving bastard to break into my chalet and steal all my money," she demanded.

The young lad behind the desk looked terrified, and I didn't blame him. You didn't mess with Mum when she was angry. He looked down at me and asked, "What colour of bracelet do you want, Andy?"

Not only did I get my bracelet, but he also gave me a big paper bag stuffed with loads of sweets and sticks of rock that had Mosney written through the

CHAPTER FIVE

middle. Enough for me to give a piece each to my brothers and sister.

Sitting on the train home, I felt so sad. Life just seemed unfair. But Mum told me to focus on all the fun we had had, and it really did make me feel better.

Other than the robbery, Butlin's was the best place ever. It was a truly special few days, and I still cherish the memories of those times with Mum.

✷✷✷

Chapter Six

GOODBYE MUM

My last memory of Mum was her heading off to a 21st birthday party. She was excited. It was around 8pm on September 9th, 2000, and I was out playing on the street, having a great time with my friends. Mum walked by all dressed up looking beautiful and said goodbye to us. She gave me a big hug and kiss, and I remember being embarrassed in front of my mates. However, I'm so glad she did as the smell of her perfume is a memory that lasts today. Little did I know that this would be the last time I'd see her alive.

After the 21st birthday party ended, which was held in a nightclub, Mum was invited to keep the celebrations going at someone's house. It was suggested she took a ride with her friend's nephew and his mate.

The nephew, who was driving, had been drinking. I've no idea if Mum was aware of this or not.

CHAPTER SIX

As they sped down Nangor Road in Clondalkin, the drunk driver lost control, crashing into a roundabout. The car, a Honda Civic, flipped over, hitting a fence which launched it into a field. Mum was thrown from the vehicle and found lying on the grass around 4am. She was rushed to Tallaght Hospital, but it was too late. She was pronounced dead, half an hour later.

Mum was only 31, leaving behind six of us. The oldest, me, was just 12, and Ryan was a baby. Six kids, from four different fathers. My five siblings knew who theirs were, but I was the only one without a dad, leaving me effectively orphaned.

This had a profound effect on me. I felt like I didn't belong anywhere or to anyone.

Mum had her flaws as a parent, and it feels disloyal to her memory to say that out loud. I know some family members will hate reading this, but I promised myself that this book would be an honest account of my life, so I'm not going to sugarcoat anything. I've spent a lifetime being gaslit by some family members all trying to tell me my childhood wasn't that bad. I think partly they are in denial, mixed in with guilt and shame for not doing more to step in and help.

Despite her shortcomings, I never doubted that Mum loved me with every fibre of her being. It was an unconditional love that I felt throughout my life.

SMELLY KID

When she couldn't feed us, I could feel her pain as deeply as my own. My relationship with Mum had matured, we would sit up late, when the little ones were asleep, just the two of us watching telly. She had started to open up to me about more grown-up things and I felt I could tell her anything. I didn't just lose a parent. Mum was my best friend.

My mother was a victim of the strict Catholic society she was born into. Birth control was frowned upon, and having sex before marriage was even worse. She fell pregnant with me when she was just a teenager on holiday, and the consequences led to shame, being shunned, and societal labels.

Mum tried her best, even though the odds were stacked against her. But what hope did she have, being a single mother, in Ireland at the age of 19 and the man in her life, John, who was supposed to be protecting her, did the opposite – getting her pregnant two more times and then abandoning her at the age of 23, with three kids to look after which he didn't support.

Now she was gone, and I felt utterly abandoned and alone.

Ryan and Dan ended up with Aunt Teresa. Connor was with his foster parents, while Patrick, Aoife, and I went to live with their dad, John.

Living with John was a nightmare. The place was filthy. Dirty dishes piled up in the sink, covered in

CHAPTER SIX

mouldy food and cigarette butts. Dog shit littered the floor. John would lash out at us tiny kids, for no reason at all.

We were all grieving for our Mammy, kids who needed love and kindness. Instead, we barely got food. John spent all day at the pub. That meant that us little ones did too. We were dragged from pub to pub. Constantly surrounded by older, drunken men. Totally inappropriate for Patrick and myself, worse for Aoife. When John was home he mainly slept. Passed out drunk on the sofa. If we wanted to do anything at home, even use the toilet or get a glass of water, we had to tiptoe so we didn't disturb him. If we did wake him, he would rage at us.

One time he caught Aoife with a cigarette and he flicked it in her face, burning her. Another time he caught her taking a sip of his whiskey and he slapped her on the face. He made us boys watch this punishment and told her that we knew he was doing the right thing.

Again, I just watched this, with anger burning inside. I wanted to help her, but how could I? I was only little myself. A neglected, scrawny kid.

Mum's side of the family tried to rescue me from John. He wasn't my birth father so he had no real claim to me. A court case ensued, and the result was that Patrick and Aoife were given to the care of their grandmother (John's mum). I went to live with my mum's brother, Uncle James, and his wife, my Aunt Margaret.

The next few years were a blur. I was a nightmare kid to look after. Of course I was! I was angry, lashing out at everyone, even those trying to help me. Life felt so unfair. No, it *was* unfair. Add puberty into the mix, with raging hormones as I entered my teens, and it was a perfect storm.

I'm definitely somewhere on the spectrum, though undiagnosed. Back then, nobody spoke of ADHD or Autism, at least not where I was. I was just labelled as "bad" and "unmanageable". I'll admit to being the latter, but I don't think I'm a bad person.

I'd last a short time with one relative before they gave up on me and I was passed to someone else in our big family. Every time this happened, I changed schools. I was moved again and again, attending 13 schools in total before finally bailing out of the educational system at just 15 years old.

For some reason Patrick and I ended up back living with John. Can't quite remember why. I think it was likely, there were no more relatives left that were willing to deal with me. I was desperate for somewhere to stay as I'd actually been sleeping rough and was struggling to survive on the streets.

Moving back with John was a terrible mistake. I was older and could understand better how much of a scumbag he actually was. I could see him taunting

CHAPTER SIX

Aoife and it made my blood boil. One night he called me from home, drunk and slurring as usual. He told me he was kicking me and Patrick out. I can't remember why. I said I'll be coming back for my stuff and again he mocked me. "You came with nothing. You are nothing. You'll leave with nothing."

I saw red. I remembered him hitting Mum and my sister and all the mental torture he had put us all through over the years. Enough was enough. I was growing up. He said to me after Mum died that I had to be a 'big boy for my brothers and sister'. Well I was gonna show him what that meant. I raced back to his place and just swung for him. Caught him unawares and hit him again and again. This carried out onto the street, causing a scene which the neighbours saw. He slammed a door at me and my arm got badly cut. He then called the police and told them all kinds of lies that led to them racing to the scene.

As the Garda diffused the situation, I tried to tell them what he had done to us, but nobody would listen. Nobody cared. I was just a bad person.
Now, Patrick and I were effectively homeless.

***

Chapter Seven

STREET RAT

—

The rain poured down, soaking us to the bone. We had no idea where we would spend the night. Just when we thought we couldn't get any more miserable, Tintin came to our rescue.

His real name was Michael, but everyone called him Tintin. He was attending a college course and receiving €125 per week from the government as a grant. The money was due in his account at midnight. He said if we waited with him, he'd help us out. True to his word, at midnight, he withdrew all his cash and bought us a Burger King. We sat there, devouring the feast.

Tintin couldn't offer us a place to stay. Instead, he generously gave us €50 to find a hostel for the night. We walked the streets, our soaked shoes squelching in the puddles. Eventually, we found a small, dingy hostel. The rooms were cramped and the beds uncomfortable, but at least we had a roof over our heads.

CHAPTER SEVEN

I've never forgotten Tintin's kindness and generosity, and he is still a treasured friend to this day.

The next day, Patrick managed to find somewhere to stay with his friend Christopher whose parents agreed to take Patrick in and look after him. As I watched Patrick leave with them, a wave of relief washed over me. At least he was safe.

Me? Well, things didn't work out so well. I was homeless, a word I had never thought I would have to use. The fear, the loneliness, the constant worry about where I would sleep and what I would eat – it was overwhelming.

A mate had an old white Opel Corsa car. During the day, I'd hang around with him as we worked on it. At night, I curled up in the backseat, the cold seeping in through the gaps in the car's body. The car provided some shelter from the howling wind and biting sleet, but it did little to keep me warm. My only possessions were the clothes I was wearing, a tattered jacket and worn jeans.

It was parked at Hardwicke Street Flats. As the nights drew on, the locals began to realise what was happening. Some would visit me at night with a flask of hot tea or soup, the warmth of their kindness a brief distraction from the biting cold. I was also given some blankets and extra thick socks. This might not seem much, but don't forget I was still carrying the label of being evicted from the Dorset Street Flats by the vigilante group. People were apprehensive to be seen to be associated with me. So I was grateful, even for those small gestures.

Living in the car lasted for about two weeks, and it was a gruelling ordeal. All my life, I had been used to being hungry. Sleeping in the freezing cold was normal to me as Mum rarely could have the heating on. What I wasn't used to, huddled in that car, was the crushing loneliness, the feeling of being utterly alone in the world. I'd lie in the car, staring at the night, wishing it would become morning and my friends would reappear. I hated being by myself, I still do. In these dark moments I couldn't stop thinking about Mum. I felt she was still connected to me and I missed her more than ever. During the day I'd got into the habit of visiting her grave and I'd sit there for hours on end just talking to her.

I didn't decide to stop living in the car. The council towed it away for not being taxed and having a valid NCT. I lost the few possessions I'd gathered, my few belongings taken to the compound.

Everything declined further after that. I was living rough on the streets. Just 15 years old. Sleeping anywhere that was dry. I'm deeply ashamed to admit this, but often the only way I could eat was by shoplifting the occasional sandwich or packet of crisps.

CHAPTER SEVEN

It was then that I discovered 24-hour internet cafes. I used to purchase a pass late at night and sit at a computer terminal, tucked away in a corner upstairs. I mastered the art of sleeping upright at the desk with my head resting on my arm. My body contorted into an unnatural position for sleep. The bright fluorescent lights flickered above me. Waves of loneliness sweeping over me. Surrounded by people but truly alone.

The truth is, I might have been living like a feral animal, but I still had some dignity. I didn't want people around me to know how bad it was. I was ashamed that I was homeless.

So I'd sit at the computer desk all night, trying to make it look like I was busy studying rather than sleeping.

I'm certain the owners of the cafe worked out what I was doing, but they just turned a blind eye, which I'm grateful for. In return, I tried not to cause a fuss or leave any mess.

I did get to meet some interesting characters. I remember this lad, Alex who would sit in the cafe watching 'Sex and the City' on DVD. He was the first gay man I recall knowing. I remember that he spoke so matter of factly about his boyfriend, and this kind of talk was all new to me. I was brought up surrounded by casual homophobia and derogatory terms like 'faggot' or 'queer' were commonplace.

Alex was a really nice guy and didn't fit the description of what I'd been taught gay people were. I really liked him.

Using Internet Cafes lasted months. Over time, I noticed a change in Alex. Every time I'd see him, he looked rougher and rougher. He wasn't homeless, just using the cafe as a regular customer. So I couldn't understand why he rarely changed his clothes. Then, one night, I took my usual place in the corner of the cafe and noticed Alex was slumped in a chair. I went over to discover his arm was bloody and saw a needle. I realised then that Alex was a heroin addict and had overdosed. An ambulance took him away, still alive, but I never saw him again after that.

I survived on the streets with just the clothes I was wearing. Occasionally, I'd see Patrick, and he would do some laundry for me at his place. But most of the time, I was unwashed and wearing filthy clothes. I rarely even had a change of underwear. Sometimes, if I had a bit of cash, I'd go to Penny's and buy the cheapest clothes and get changed in a toilet, binning my old stuff. Life was grim.

Then I met Clayton. He was a friend of my cousins, and we hit it off right away. He immediately offered me a place to stay, crashing in his room, which was a huge relief. We had a lot in common. Like me, he'd had a tough childhood and had recently gotten out of a youth detention centre. We spent every day

CHAPTER SEVEN

together, just wandering the streets. Any money we could scrape together usually went towards a few cans of cheap booze.

I dabbled in drugs during this time, desperate for anything that could brighten the bleakness of my existence. Cannabis made me sick, its potent effects sending me into a spiral of nausea and discomfort. Ecstasy, on the other hand, unleashed a torrent of energy, making me feel more alive than ever before. I wasn't remotely tempted by heroin, even though it was freely available. That drug was responsible for me losing my home at Dorset Street Flats. I hated everything to do with it.

Clayton and I were inseparable. He was more than a close friend. He felt like a brother, a constant source of support. He seemed to understand, like nobody else, the depths of my pain and the scars of my past. Though I never dwelled on my suffering, Clayton knew what it was like to be the odd kid out, the one everyone picked on. We found strength and determination in each other, a shared spirit that made us feel invincible.

Of course, typical of my life, our time living together was cut short. Clayton's mum hadn't been paying the rent, and they lost their flat. Once again I was back on the streets.

The only hostel I could afford was a cramped, stuffy affair. The air was thick with the stench of sweat and stale beer. Eight of us, six burly Polish truck drivers, one American guy and me, a scrawny teenager, were crammed into a single dormitory filled with bunk beds. The snoring and farting were a constant noise, lulling me into an uneasy sleep.

One night, a commotion erupted. I could hear shouts and grunts and the sound of fists connecting with flesh. A sense of dread washed over me as I realised something bad was happening. Fear gripped me, as I lay still in my bunk. I tried to ignore the noise, pretending it wasn't happening, but the din was too much. I lay there, my heart pounding in my chest, desperately trying to fall asleep and wishing I was invisible.

In the morning, one of the men woke me up, his face filled with concern. He pointed to the corner, and I saw one of the guys from last night, the American man, lying in an unnatural position. His body was stiff, his skin a ghastly grey.

The Irish tradition of having open coffins in homes had prepared me for the sight of death and I knew that guy was deceased. As the police arrived, I answered their questions and made my exit as quickly as possible, my heart pounding in my chest.

The incident shook me to my core, I needed to get my life back on track.

Aunty Linda came to the rescue. Concerned about our situation, she took Patrick and me to social

CHAPTER SEVEN

services. She argued our case, insisting that we should be treated as adults despite my age. I don't know all the details, but I believe she mentioned that, as an orphan, I was effectively a 'ward of the state'. Linda can be incredibly determined, and she wore them down. Eventually, they agreed to provide me with a living allowance and housing benefit, recognising the unique circumstances of our situation.

They found a flat for Patrick and me to live in and even provided some basic furniture and clothes. It felt so good to finally have a place of my own!

As a result of my mum's death, each of us siblings received some insurance money that was due to be paid out on our 18th birthdays. I was struggling to manage solely on the benefits and I was determined to get some money earlier. I went to court and convinced a judge to grant me a partial payment at the age of 17. As a 'ward of the state', they had some responsibility for me, and they agreed. They believed my tale that I needed to buy a car in order to work.

I received €19,000 in my bank account, but it took several meetings and explanations before the bank allowed me to withdraw it all. After everything I'd been through, I didn't trust anyone, not even a bank. So I demanded it all in cash. I felt like the richest man alive! I immediately took Patrick shopping, buying my first-ever pair of branded trainers: Air Jordans. We also stayed at a posh hotel for a few nights, indulging in luxurious meals. Eating my first-ever proper steak is a memory I'll never forget. The spending continued as I just had fun living the good life.

But the money was fast dwindling, and the only thing I wanted to do with what was left was to get myself out of Dublin.

I left half the remaining cash with Patrick and raced over to where Clayton was staying. Unfortunately, he didn't have a passport; however, his stepfather did. A middle-aged man we called Paddywack! Late that night, we went straight to Dublin airport. The only flight available was to Cork. Even though it was still within Ireland, I said we should take that flight because I didn't want to go home. When we arrived in Cork, we discovered the next available flight was heading to Heraklion in Crete.

I had the best two weeks ever! Paddy was surprisingly good company. We rented a cheap apartment. Paddy very much enjoyed the raki, a strong local spirit. I enjoyed the clubs and the girls! I was a late developer when it came to the opposite sex, and there will be more about that later. But Crete certainly opened my eyes.

I was definitely showing off, throwing my money around like it was confetti. But jeez, did I have fun! That holiday gave me a taste of a different life. For the first time ever, I felt respected by people rather than looked down on.

CHAPTER SEVEN

I didn't stop partying until I'd spent everything I had. The problem was, we didn't have flights home. So, I called Patrick to ask him to do a Western Union transfer for me. He said he would, but then I couldn't get hold of him. I called and called, using the remaining coins I had, stuck at the airport. Eventually, he answered and confessed he had taken a group of lads to Liverpool and spent all of my cash. Everything! I was furious. I couldn't get home. Patrick told me he would sort something, and I had no choice but to trust him. We slept at the airport, and in the morning, he had transferred over €300.

It wasn't enough to fly to Dublin, but we got a flight to Belfast and took the coach home from there.

When I turned 18, I got the rest of my insurance money. It didn't last long. I took Patrick to Florida and we had a superb time, visiting all the theme parks. We got to do stuff that as a child growing up felt was never for the likes of us.

Maybe I should have invested my money in a flat or something responsible, but I just wanted a taste of the simple things that most people took for granted.

Back in Dublin, Patrick told me about a scheme where you could get working visas to Australia. I instantly knew that's what I wanted. I had to get as far away from Dublin as possible, and Australia ticked that box. I applied, and surprisingly, the visa turned up two days later. By this time, I had a girlfriend,

Rachel. She was upset I was leaving but understood. She said she would come out with me for the first couple of weeks. Clayton came to the airport to wave us goodbye. Nobody else knew I was going, not even Patrick. He had his own insurance money by this time and was okay.

It was time to start a whole new life down under. Goodbye, Dublin.

***

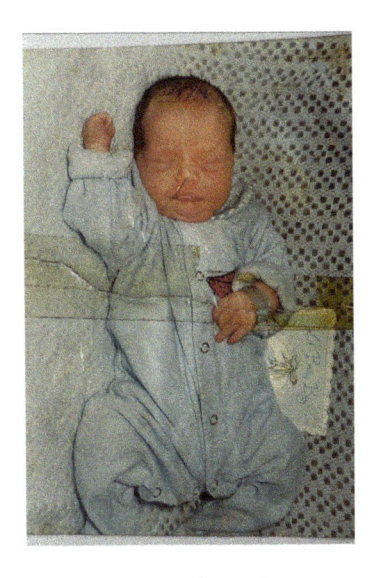

First ever photo of me ripped in half by John

Me and Mum

Me and my Nanny Rose at her house

My first birthday

Proud older brother to new baby Patrick

Me and Patrick

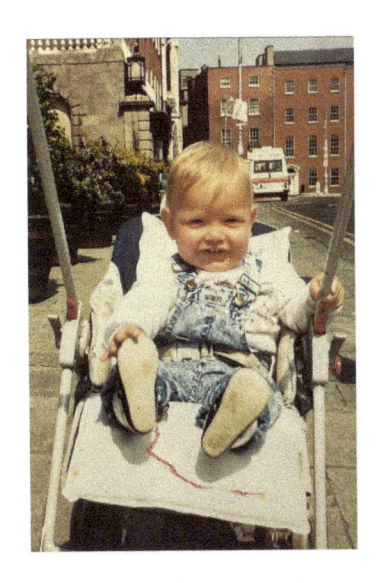

Me in my buggy outside Colaiste Mhuire

Excited to board the train for Sunshine House

Day out with Mum at the duck pond

Santa came to my school

Me giggling with Mum and Patrick

Me and Patrick, St Paddy's Day

Me and Patrick in our flat in Dorset Street before getting evicted by the mob

The 'mob'

*Me and my school friend Cathal.
Photo taken by teacher Brian*

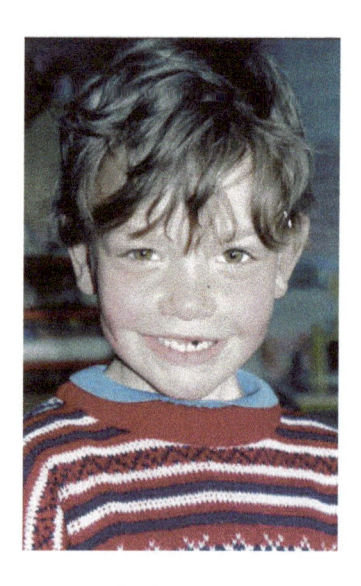

*In school smiling with
my black teeth*

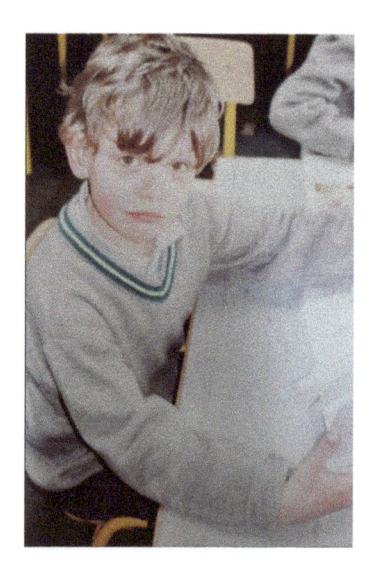

Brian's class 1996

Our last Christmas with Mum

Me, my sister Aoife and friends digging holes on Balbriggan beach at Sunshine House

Me, Brian and some kids doing a sandcastle competition at Sunshine House

Me and Mum at Butlin's

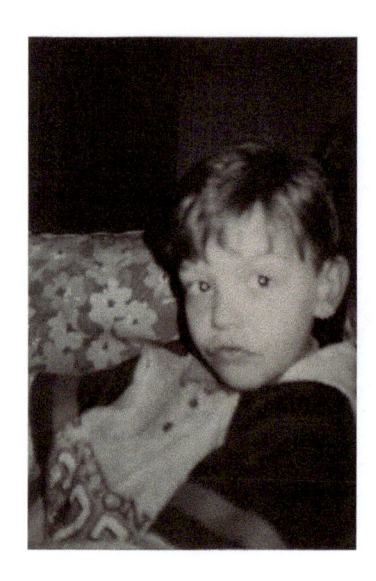

Posing for Mum *Concentrating on my colouring in*

From right to left. Dan, me, friend Steven, Aoife, friend Karl playing outside our house in Croke Villas

Little Andy painting

Me, Aoife and Patrick posing for a photo the day before Mum died

All my siblings together at Auntie Teresa's house, not long after Mum died

All the siblings together to mark the first anniversary of Mum's death

Me and baby brother Ryan

Mum

Mum

Photo from Mum's gravestone

Chapter Eight

REBORN

As my feet touched the warm Australian ground as I stepped off the plane, I felt a sense of being reborn. This was my chance to start all over. The first thing I saw when I exited Sydney airport were signs advertising accommodation in an area called Kings Cross. So that's where I asked the taxi driver to take us. He gave me a bit of a 'knowing wink', which I didn't quite understand at the time. Once we arrived, though, it all became clear.

Kings Cross, a once well-to-do neighbourhood, had transformed into a notorious red-light district. Its reputation as 'Sin City' was well-deserved, with a vibrant nightlife scene filled with strip clubs, casinos, and bars that stayed open until the small hours of the morning. The area was also known for its drug trade, and the streets were often bustling with a mix of tourists, locals, and people seeking illicit pleasures and I felt right at home.

SMELLY KID

Rachel and I checked into a hostel and soon got chatting with some backpackers. I was told that if I wanted any labouring work, I needed to get myself a 'white card'. It was a one-day course, focusing on health and safety at work. I got booked on immediately, attending the following day.

On the course, I got chatting to a lad who knew of a job, and next day I was employed as a labourer digging up land near the dock.

This was proper hard physical graft, something that I wasn't used to. Let's be honest, I was a malnourished and pretty weak teenager who had never done a full day's work in his life. Something else I wasn't used to, coming from Dublin, was the sun! I managed to get heatstroke on my first day and was sick as a dog. Sweat drenched my clothes, and my head throbbed. I didn't say anything to my co-workers.

All my life, I'd been labelled. Scum. Vermin. Stinky. Poor. Scrounger. And each label stung, leaving an invisible scar on my heart. As a child, I felt trapped, not knowing anything different, forced to accept these labels as my reality. How could I, back then, a little kid, possibly prove differently?

But here in Australia, a flicker of defiance ignited within me. I knew I was more than the 'low-life' these labels reduced me to. Circumstances had pushed me down a dark path, led me to make some

CHAPTER EIGHT

bad choices, but deep down, I knew I wasn't a bad person. The real me, the person I longed to be, was buried beneath the weight of shame and judgement. I could never have found that person, had I remained in Ireland.

I had a reputation, and the only way to shake that had been to leave. I'm convinced now, that if I hadn't left Ireland when I did, I would have continued on a destructive journey that would have led to prison or an early death.

The thought of it sent a shiver down my spine, even under the scorching Australian sun. Leaving Dublin and everything I knew, might have been risky, but it was the lifeline I needed. In Sydney, my past was a distant echo, and I could finally find the person I'd always wanted to be.

Despite feeling rough with sunstroke, I was determined to drag myself back to work the following day. The sun beat down relentlessly, my skin prickling with sunburn, my muscles aching from yesterday's exertion. But I wasn't going to let a little discomfort derail me. I slapped on a hat, slathered on sunscreen, and filled my water bottle to the brim. I was going to make this work, one sweaty, sun-drenched day at a time.

I stuck at that job, earned some cash, but more importantly, earned the respect of my co-workers. Other men thought I was an okay guy to be around.

SMELLY KID

They even said I was a grafter and that made me feel, for the first time, like I was one of them.

The first two weeks flew by. Rachel went sightseeing during the days I was working, and we explored the city together at night. It soon became time for her to leave, which was upsetting for both of us. I totally understood, though. Her life was back in Ireland, and I appreciated her helping to get me settled.

In other news, Patrick's visa had finally come through! He was also on his way over, flying into Brisbane.

I decided to join him there and said goodbye to my new pals in Sydney, hopping on a flight to be reunited with my brother. We stayed in a hostel for a while, then Patrick went to stay with his uncle in Melbourne.

I got another labouring job for a father & son construction company. Things went well, and I got a company van to drive. I absorbed everything I was shown and learned a lot about the trade and was made to feel like a valued member of the team. Over time, I'd open up a little about my past. I never really intended to talk about it, but when you are stuck on a building site all day, you get to know each other pretty well, and I'd answer any questions I was asked. One way that my ADHD presents itself is that I can't tell lies. Another way is that I start speaking

CHAPTER EIGHT

before my brain is in gear. There is no filter. So, when I'm asked a question, I answer. Often divulging way more details than I ever intended to!

The firm employed this painter, Ted, from New Zealand. Now Ted was pretty wild and worked very quickly. Extraordinarily fast. Like a painting machine! Very often, the owners of the homes we were renovating would vacate and stay with family whilst we were working. When this happened, Ted would stay and paint all through the night. I soon discovered his overnight work was fuelled by his addiction to Crystal Meth, locally known as 'Ice'. He was a full-blown addict, and everyone at work knew. On one job, a camera and some cash went missing from the house. It could only reasonably have been myself or Ted that stole it, and I knew it wasn't me. However, I got the blame.

"You can't come back until those items are returned," my boss said.

I was so upset. I realised then that my past was still affecting me. My boss chose to believe the Irish toe-rag was a thief rather than the junkie who had an expensive addiction to fund.

The injustice of it burned hotter than the midday sun. I'd fought so hard to shed the labels of my past, to prove I was more than the smelly kid from Dorset Street Flats. Yet, here I was, once again being judged for who I'd been, not who I'd become. But I wouldn't let this setback break me. I held my head high, met my boss's gaze, and said, "I didn't take anything. But I understand your decision."

I walked away, the weight of his accusation heavy on my shoulders, but with my head held high. It was then that I met Keith, an inspirational guy who instantly took me under his wing. I was meant to be just his labourer, but he went above and beyond, teaching me the skills of the building trade which I still use today. Recognising my loneliness and the fact that I had nowhere else to go that Christmas, Keith extended a heartwarming invitation: to spend the holiday with his family. It was an act of generosity he didn't have to offer, and I was deeply touched by his kindness. Having a full turkey dinner in the hot sunshine whilst wearing a party hat and pulling crackers, followed by us all going surfing at Queensland's Gold Coast, Surfers Paradise, was the oddest experience, but one of my fondest Christmas memories to this day.

I understand this might not seem like much, but being treated by Keith and his family like a normal human being who had some value meant everything to me. It made me realise that maybe I had something to offer this world after all.

I had been staying at this hostel and found myself in the middle of a fight that I didn't start. Once again, exactly like my school years, I got punished

CHAPTER EIGHT

for defending myself and was asked to leave. Seeing my predicament, Keith stepped in and generously offered to put down a deposit for a flat for Patrick and me to live in. Patrick had returned from his uncle's to join me at this point. However, not long after we moved in, Patrick randomly took himself off to Thailand, initially for a week but ended up staying for six months, leaving me struggling to pay the rent on my own as he was supposed to be contributing.

In the end, I just couldn't manage that and had to move out. I parted ways with Keith on the best terms and decided to explore a different part of Australia.

All these life experiences led me to realise that I just couldn't depend on anyone, even family, and if I wanted to progress in life I needed to be fully independent.

I ended up in Melbourne and got myself a job as an industrial window cleaner, which I surprisingly enjoyed. The job required early starts and early finishes, which suited me as I'm a bit of a live-wire in the mornings. I was working with these older chaps and I used to enjoy just listening to their tales in the van driving into work each day. It wasn't anything extraordinary they were telling me – just about their everyday home lives with family. What seemed normal to them was anything but to me, and I sat there like a sponge, just soaking up how regular people lived.

SMELLY KID

One morning on the way into work, I got a call from Leon, a mate from Dublin.

"Hey bro, did you hear about Clayton?" he asked.

"Yes, it's his birthday; I was only messaging with him last night.

"Is everything ok?"

"I'm so sorry, Andy, but Clayton died last night of an overdose."

I was utterly numb. I actually continued at work and didn't say anything to the guys. I didn't have the words to say it out loud. I've no idea how I got through that day, but I remember just going home and reading his last messages, feeling totally empty and sobbing till there was nothing left. I barely remember ever crying before. It felt like a lifetime of grief just came out. Last night I had a best mate. His name was Clayton and I truly loved him like any brother I had, maybe more so. Today he was gone.

I was on the phone to Aunty Linda arranging to go home for his funeral but she talked me out of it. "Clayton is gone, Andy, you coming back to Dublin won't change that. Your life is in Australia for now and Clayton wouldn't want you to give that all up," she said.

I tried to argue but I knew deep down she was right.

I marked Clayton's life by getting his name tattooed on my upper arm and "Life goes on" on

CHAPTER EIGHT

my forearm. It was from the Tupac song that we both used to play over and over, and it seemed so appropriate.

Clayton, my friend, I made sure life went on and I'm living it to the absolute max for the both of us.

Even though I'd never touched drugs since leaving Dublin anyway, from that moment on I vowed never to touch a drug in my life. I hate everything to do with their evil and what they represent. I won't be around anyone who uses them. I barely even drink alcohol and I've never smoked.

I was now determined to make Australia my home. By this time Rachel and I had mutually agreed to end our relationship, and I was pretty loved up with Emma who worked in a bank – I had met her when collecting my wages. Emma was also a singer and I used to enjoy going with her to gigs.

I had somewhere nice to stay, a steady job, lots of mates and a stunning girlfriend. Then my visa ran out. Initially I buried my head in the sand about it and overstayed for a few weeks but eventually I had to face up to it and visited the embassy. I told them it would take me five weeks to work and save enough for my flight home and they took pity on me and gave me that extension.

During those five weeks I met some English lads on leave from the Army. I thought their life sounded so cool and they put me in touch with Nicky, an army recruitment officer based in London. I passed preliminary suitability checks, and she arranged an interview for me in an office in Leicester Square.

I was absolutely gutted to be leaving Australia. It felt like home to me, and I was the happiest I'd ever been in my life. However, the five weeks flew by and I saved enough to buy a one-way ticket to London Heathrow.

British Army, here I come!

***

Chapter Nine

"GAY FOR PAY"

—

"Would you stand in front of MY Queen, with those stars tattooed on your neck?" the army recruitment officer asked me with a voice that could barely hide his disgust at my appearance.

I was standing there trembling, feeling belittled and it was at that moment, surrounded by polished boots and crisp uniforms, that I realised an Army career was not for me.

I hadn't thought this through. A lifetime of being spoken down to, had left me fragile. Too fragile for this.

Mumbling an excuse, I quickly left with the London air slapping my face as I stumbled out into Leicester Square. Just over 24 hours ago I had an amazing life in Australia, with a job, friends and a lovely girlfriend, and now that was all gone and once again I was utterly on my own. I'd never felt as lost and lonely as I did in that moment. How can you be surrounded by people and yet feel invisible? Most of my money had gone on the flight. What little I had left was prioritised for a hostel.

I had no idea what I was going to do other than being certain I wasn't returning to Dublin.

I found a hostel and soon made a friend, Sidney, a photographer from the Philippines. We spent our days exploring London while he took pictures.

After two weeks of hanging out together, we were waiting for a bus at Westfield Shopping Centre, and Sidney quietly mumbled, "Andy, you know I'm gay, don't you?"

I was sure I'd misheard. "You are what?" I asked, surprised.

"Well, I'm gay, Andy," he confirmed.

I felt so confused. I'd been chatting non-stop about girls, and Sidney had been actively participating in those conversations. In fact, we were out that day with two gorgeous Swedish women we'd met at the hostel. I'd thought we both had a chance!

"Why didn't you say something earlier?" I asked him.

"Well, I thought you might beat me up or something," Sidney admitted, his face clearly concerned.

"Look, pal, I don't care one little bit. Who am I to judge anyone?" I reassured him.

CHAPTER NINE

Just then, the girls returned, and my ADHD brain took over. "Hey, did you know Sidney was gay?" I blurted out.

"Yes, of course we did. It's pretty obvious," they replied with a smile.

That's when I learned about "gaydar", and I definitely don't have it! Still don't.

Other than Alex from the internet cafe in Dublin, Sidney was the first openly gay person I really knew. With Alex, I'd simply listened when he shared his experiences. With Sidney, it was different. I was fascinated and wanted to know every detail, from his sex life to how he met guys. My main concern, though, was that he might be missing out on wonderful sexual intimacy with women. When I asked if he was absolutely certain he was gay, he just laughed at my silliness and assured me he wasn't missing out on anything!

I'd developed a fondness for the gym while in Australia and was eager to continue my fitness journey in London. Having always been skinny I was thoroughly enjoying the process of building muscle. The girls seemed to appreciate it too, making it a win-win situation! The hostel had a deal with a local gym. I eagerly took advantage of it and spent countless hours there. It was a welcoming environment, which, unlike the hostel, provided endless hot showers, a definite plus! It was at this gym that I made another friend, Bailey. He was from South Africa and represented everything I aspired to be. His hair was flawless, his physique was sculpted, he was undeniably handsome, and was oozing this quiet confidence. The girls flocked to him like moths to a flame. I was completely in awe.

Bailey and I quickly became close. He loved to party, which often led to intimate encounters with stunning women. I thoroughly enjoyed becoming a part of that, though I often struggled to keep up financially.

One evening, I introduced Bailey to Sidney, and we all headed to a bar. Everyone seemed to be getting along famously. However, upon returning from the toilet, I noticed an awkward silence between them. It felt as if I'd interrupted a private conversation. Discreetly, I took my seat, pretending not to have noticed. Just kidding! My ADHD brain kicked in, and I blurted out, "Hey, what were you two talking about that I wasn't supposed to hear?"

Their faces turned red, and neither uttered a word. The silence stretched on until Bailey finally said to Sidney, "Okay, you can tell him."

Sidney replied hesitantly, "Are you absolutely certain?"

They both looked incredibly uncomfortable.

Exasperated, I exclaimed, "For fuck's sake, what could it possibly be that's such a big deal?"

CHAPTER NINE

"Bailey's a gay porn star," Sidney blurted out.

"I'm not gay," Bailey snapped back, clearly wanting to clarify. "I've filmed porn for a gay website."

I was completely bewildered.

"Bailey, I've literally seen you making out with girls." (Hostels offer zero privacy.) "How can you be gay?"

"I'm not gay," Bailey repeated, his voice laced with frustration.

"Bailey, I honestly don't care if you are gay," I said, smirking, enjoying his discomfort as Bailey squirmed in his chair.

"I'm not gay." He was becoming more wound up.

"Ok, can someone please explain what the hell is going on?" I pleaded, a wide grin spreading across my face.

And then, the truth came out. I'll rephrase that. No one "came out", but Bailey shared his secret.

He'd been earning money by performing for a website called 'EnglishLads' It was a subscription-based site catering to gay men, specialising in showcasing attractive, typically straight guys who were willing to perform for a gay audience. The work ranged from solo scenes involving, well, self-pleasure, to collaborations with other models where they'd receive higher pay for 'pushing boundaries' with each other. This was also known as going 'gay for pay'.

Sidney, the dirty dog, had a subscription to EnglishLads and recognised Bailey. Hence their hushed conversation while I was in the toilet.

Bailey turned to me and said, "Look, I know this is a lot to take in. Do you have any questions?"

"Yes," I replied without hesitation. "How much?"

"You don't think any less of me?" Bailey inquired.

"Of course not," I assured him. "I think it sounds like a fantastic way to make money!"

"So, how much?" I asked again.

Bailey grinned. "Well, I've seen you in the showers, mate. It's impossible to miss. It's absolutely massive. Forget what I can earn; with your 'monster', you could be a millionaire!"

And that, dear readers, marked the beginning of an entirely new chapter in my life.

✷✷✷

Chapter Ten

"LOSING MY VIRGINITY"

—

DEAR READER,

This chapter comes with a warning as it contains descriptions of my early sexual development. So, if you are family or just generally uncomfortable with such topics, you may wish to skip to the next part. Saying that, the rest of the book is likely to contain descriptions of a sexual nature, as let's be honest, this is the story of an adult content creator.

I'm going to be as considerate as possible with my language. However, I'm also not going to hold back on describing what I do in the adult industry and what led me to do it.

I'm also writing this, aware that this information and detail will be interesting to those who have followed my career. So, I have this fine balancing act of giving my fans the juicy details, whilst considering who else might be reading.

SMELLY KID

So, I guess I need to start by answering a question I've been asked most often: "When did I first realise I was blessed in the trouser department?"

Well, I didn't have any idea at all that I was different from other lads until I was about 15 years old. You see, my brothers, to some degree, are similar, so I just thought I was normal. I really don't remember thinking about my 'size' much at all. I was a fairly late developer when it came to anything sexual or even being sexually aware.

But when I was about 15, I was hanging out with some mates in the park, and I was dared to go into the local convenience store, get my willy out, slap it on the deli counter, and say, "Put that in a roll". So I did, and my friends all just gasped and seemed to be very impressed! I felt very confused, and it was only when they showed me what "normal" looks like, I became aware of just how different I was.

I also just want to point out that as I remember this story, I also feel some shame about exposing myself as I did in the shop. I don't tell that tale with a sense of pride. I'm a very different person now and understand just how inappropriate it was and that consent is everything.

But yes, that was how I discovered that I had a big dick!

The other "attribute" that I'm known for is my ejaculation! It's often referred to as a fountain, often

CHAPTER TEN

with more than ten very powerful "spurts"!

Again, this has always been normal for me from when I started doing that thing that is supposed to make you go blind. If that tale were true, I'd have a white stick and a dog by now, but I'm pleased to report I still have 20:20 vision. It was only when I did my first paid shoot for EnglishLads that I became aware I didn't spurt like most other guys... but more about EnglishLads later.

I remember watching movies like American Pie when the guy was clearly about to jerk off and having some tissue on standby and just being so confused as to its purpose. I realise now it was to "mop up" afterwards. Well, a tissue would never work for me! I'd need an entire bath towel!

Once my friends knew about how blessed I was, they were always demanding I get it out and show it off, and I'll be honest, I really enjoyed the attention. I clearly still do.

I remember lads at school talking about "wanking", listening to audio porn, and I just had no idea what "wanking" was. I was so innocent.

I found a VHS at one of my uncle's, and it was a porno! This couple were going at it in a bakery, I seem to recall! I'm so tempted to make baking innuendos, but I'm not that childish... Or maybe I am...

Anyway, this movie really got my attention. Well, I soon developed a "stiff peak", and I soon figured out what this "wanking" was all about. In fact, watching those 'Belgian buns' jiggling around definitely created a 'cream horn' and resulted in me "icing the cake". Not just once whilst enjoying the movie, but many times! I haven't really stopped since!

I had my first kiss when I was 14. With a cute girl in the car park of a church. I'm such a romantic! I had no idea what to do. My friends had been egging me on, saying we needed to put our tongues in each other's mouths, but that sounded weird. In the end, I just confessed it was my first time, and she said, "Don't worry, I'll show you what to do," and she took the lead.

It felt magical!

That definitely awakened something in me, but I was still pretty innocent, and for the next few years, I was only kissing girls, and if I was really lucky, I might get to squeeze a boob.

I was never shy about nudity or anything like that – growing up as I did; there was very little privacy at home.

So, I was always happy to whip it out on demand and was often asked to do so. I do remember me and some mates on a train journey decided to have a wanking competition to see who could "finish" first. Again, I'm aware how inappropriate that is now, but we were just kids learning about ourselves, and it was an otherwise empty carriage!

CHAPTER TEN

I was 17 when I finally lost my virginity. The setting wasn't exactly romantic – Hardwicke Street Flats – but the girl was someone special. Stacy. We were tight, the kind of friends who'd go out partying, get a bit tipsy, and end up snogging each other silly. All good fun, nothing serious. She had a boyfriend, and I was just enjoying being young and free.

One night, we were babysitting for Stacy's aunt. The aunt asked me to help put together some bunk beds and said I could crash there afterwards. We got the beds built; it was late, around 1am, and we ended up in her aunt's bed.

We started messing about, kissing, the usual drunken foreplay. Then, out of the blue, Stacy says, "If you can make me climax, we can have sex."

Now, Stacy had only done it once before, and I was a virgin. I was nervous as hell.

"How am I supposed to do that?" I asked, clueless.

"Figure it out," she said.

And so we did. It was probably terrible. I had no idea what I was doing. She was hurting, and I felt so awkward. The whole experience was clumsy and fumbling, but we got the job done. It was about two in the morning.

Afterwards, I decided to head home. I was feeling ecstatic. Over the moon. I'd just lost my virginity! I was a man now!

SMELLY KID

My house was about five, maybe ten miles away. I walked. It took hours, but I didn't care. I was strolling the streets at three in the morning, grinning like an idiot. I was whistling and singing songs. I said hello to the bin men as they were doing their rounds, maybe expecting a pat on the back. They must've thought I was crazy, but I didn't care. I'd just lost my virginity.

And that, my friends, is how it happened. And let me tell you, it hasn't stopped since then.

✱✱✱

Chapter Eleven

"BORN FOR PORN"

Bailey's revelation, that he was earning money performing for a gay audience on an adult website, had left my brain working overtime. The idea of a guy making a living showcasing his, well, talents, was a concept I'd never considered. At the time, I was doing casual work in demolition, a back-breaking job that paid a measly £5 an hour. I was desperate for a way out, a chance to build a future for myself that didn't involve dust, sweat, and the constant risk of injury. The prospect of a new path, one paved with possibilities and financial freedom, was too tempting to ignore.

With Bailey's connections at the website 'EnglishLads', things moved quickly. I sent over some photos – headshots, full-body shots, and yes, even some naked ones. It felt strange, exposing myself like that, but a wave of confidence washed over me.

SMELLY KID

I'd often been told that I had something unique in my underwear; it had never crossed my mind that it could be something valuable.

Anything had to be better than demolition.

The next day, I found myself at the EnglishLads headquarters, a sprawling mansion in the heart of Angel, North London. Nick, the owner, and his assistant, Zach, greeted me warmly. They explained the process, offering me food and reassurance. It would be a two-part shoot: photos first, then a video, each paying a handsome £300.

Nervousness mingled with excitement as I was led to a white backdrop in a studio. The lights were harsh, and I felt a wave of self-consciousness. Nick gave me instructions, posing me in different ways to highlight my physique.

As I got into the groove, I found myself quite enjoying the attention.

Once Nick had captured all my poses, he asked me if I was ready to climax. I said that I could 'let go' any time, and he signalled that he was ready.

I don't think it was like anything they had ever experienced before. A torrent erupted, catching Nick and Zach completely off guard. The force of it left them speechless for a moment as Nick was frantically hitting the shutter on the camera, trying to capture as much as possible.

CHAPTER ELEVEN

The problem was, it sprayed beyond the set, covering a lot of their filming gear.

As they scrambled to clean up the mess, their faces a mixture of astonishment and amusement, I felt rather embarrassed, with a surge of heat rising to my cheeks. But Nick simply slapped me on the back and laughed. "Bloody hell, Andy," he said. "We weren't expecting that!"

"Yeah," Zach chimed in, wiping down the backdrop with a towel. "You made one hell of a mess, mate. With your size and now this, you really have something unique going on."

I couldn't help but grin. In that moment, I knew I had something special to offer. The embarrassment faded, replaced by a sense of possibility.

The rest of the shoot went smoothly, though Nick kept throwing me cheeky glances. They clearly saw the potential in me, and I was eager to explore it further.

Before I left, they invited me back the next day for another shoot. Same kind of deal, but wearing different clothes in a different setting. I then got invited back again a few days later to film with Bailey.

This third time, though, was different. Bailey and I were asked to perform side by side on the same bed. Not touching, Nick clarified, but close enough for the camera to capture both of us. A wave of awkwardness washed over me. Doing it solo was

SMELLY KID

one thing, but with Bailey beside me felt different. I wasn't even sure I'd be able to 'perform'.

Bailey was also apprehensive. The reality was that Nick had run out of ideas for either of us to work solo. Performing together put a new spin on it and gave us the opportunity to earn more cash, which Bailey and I both needed.

So, I gave him a reassuring wink as we stripped down and took our positions. It was a strange mix. I was still in awe of how perfect Bailey looked, feeling slightly inadequate. However, I know he felt something similar about the size of my dick compared to his. Not that he was particularly lacking in any way, but I'm aware my unusual size would make most guys feel self-conscious.

Nick started the camera and gave us some direction. I stole a glance at Bailey, his eyes closed, his expression a mix of concentration and pleasure. As I approached my climax, I couldn't help but feel a strange mix of self-consciousness and exhilaration. And then it happened. The force of my release took even me by surprise, and a jet of fluid arced through the air, landing a few inches from Bailey's leg.

I froze, mortified. Bailey's eyes snapped open, and he stared at the white stain on the sheet, then back at me. I hadn't finished though, and he actually had to shuffle out of the way as I erupted.

CHAPTER ELEVEN

"Well, well, well," he said. "Someone's got a bit of a cannon, haven't they?"

"Sorry, mate," I mumbled, trying to wipe away the evidence with my hand.

Despite the awkwardness, the shoot went well, and we were both handsomely rewarded for our efforts. In my first week, I'd earned £1,800 – more than I'd ever made in my life. Compared to my measly £5 an hour doing demolition, this was a fortune.

I quickly became the new face of EnglishLads, attending events and shoots. Nick saw my potential, and I became his golden boy, his cash cow.

I was on a roll, exploring these new opportunities. I soon realised there was only so much work Nick could offer me, so I actively searched for other websites to do similar work.

The money was flowing, and I was finally experiencing a taste of the life I'd always craved. It was a far cry from the streets of Dublin, and I was determined to make the most of it.

I was no longer Andy the orphan, Andy the scrounger, Andy the nobody. I was now Andy Lee, the rising star of the adult industry, and I was just getting started.

✳✳✳

Chapter Twelve

"BEYOND THE PAYWALL"

I soon realised there was a limit to what I could achieve on adult websites catering to gay men who enjoyed watching masculine straight guys like me perform. This work often involved crossing lines I wasn't prepared to cross.

Let me explain how it worked.

Websites like EnglishLads would put up these modelling ads that looked totally innocent, like something any bloke could do. They'd target regular lads needing some extra cash, even popping up in the 'labouring jobs' section of those classified ad websites. So, some fellas might be looking for a day's work on a building site, stumble across these ads, and think, "Why not? Bit of easy money, no harm in that".

The initial photo shoot might be simple: posing in sportswear – maybe rugby kit or speedos – nothing too revealing. The guys would show up nervous

CHAPTER TWELVE

but usually leave with a positive experience and decent money. That's how Bailey's first shoot with Nick went.

Then came the next offer: more money to return for a fully nude shoot. Many would be tempted, having already had a good experience. If they hesitated, they'd be told they wouldn't even need to get an erection.

Let's be honest. If the original ad had been for a nude shoot, most wouldn't have bothered. But showing off their physique in their underwear felt okay.

So after having had an ok experience the first time around, they'd return to do the nude shoot, be treated well, get paid, and think, "Easy money".

Next, they'd get offered even more to return and push boundaries. Maybe jerking off on camera. By this point, they'd reason, "Well, I've already shown my bits, so what's the harm in getting hard?"

The next offer might be receiving a sensual massage from another guy – fully nude, with their bare buttocks being massaged, but no touching of their penis.

After that, the suggestion could be jerking off alongside another guy, like Bailey and I did. Or another massage, this time with a "happy ending".

All the while, subscribers watched these lads push their limits. It was like a journey, everyone eager to see how far each new lad would go.

Nick was always pushing for more explicit content, each shoot crossing a new line for more cash.

Some straight guys would even end up having sex with another man – the ultimate boundary, the most financially rewarding, yet also the most personally challenging.

I want to be clear: I don't judge how websites like EnglishLads operated. Business is business, and the models had free choice. But inevitably, some guys prioritised quick cash over their boundaries, leading to regrets.

My situation was different. Thanks to my unusually large member, I was often asked to do multiple solo shoots, more than most other lads got to do. Directors got creative, for example, filming me jerking off in the shower one time, then on a rooftop terrace the next.

I was constantly asked to push sexual boundaries with other men, and I always said no. I turned down tens of thousands of pounds, even when skint. Something inside me said I'd regret it, and I'm glad I listened.

The truth is, if I'd crossed those lines years ago, the money would be spent. Gone. But the website owner? They'd still own the content and would still be raking it in today off my earlier work.

CHAPTER TWELVE

My refusal to push certain boundaries limited my earnings. I'd find a new website, film until they ran out of ideas within my limitations, then move on to a different studio.

Some might wonder why I didn't do straight porn. Simple answer: it wasn't available. Most male/female adult movies focused on the woman rather than the guy. Often, the male performer was also the director. There were few chances for straight, UK-based males to make adult movies with women.

I was always hustling for more work. I'd already filmed that scene with Bailey and was okay doing more like that. I figured if I found new lads wanting to earn cash, it'd benefit both of us. If I introduced them to directors, like Bailey did for me, I'd often join them on shoots, meaning more work and money for me. Win-win.

Then I discovered sensual wrestling. Chris Geary, a director specialising in it, was looking for models. After a chat, I felt he was someone I could work with.

I told Bailey, and he was up for it. Looking back, our roles had reversed. I was the one talking to directors, making connections, finding work. I soon realised these directors often had a tough time; many lads were unreliable or had bad attitudes.

This baffled me. Why make life harder? I figured, if I said I'd do a job, I'd do it right. No messing about. I'd be on time, bring what they asked for. If they

SMELLY KID

needed work trousers or boots for a shoot, I'd bring them. After my life being a struggle, this was a chance to be good at something, and I was good at making porn!

Even though I'm not gay, I tried to see things from a gay audience's perspective. I knew that the harder I worked, the more they'd enjoy it, and the more they'd want me back. It confused me that not all models thought this way. Some were too focused on the quick cash, not on making good content with the director.

The wrestling was silly but fun! It was filmed in a massive paddling pool. Chris had gathered a bunch of fit, handsome lads.

The first scene had us in Speedos, slathered in baby oil, wrestling in pairs. We'd grapple, sliding all over. My competitive side kicked in; I didn't want to lose. Problem was, all the guys felt the same, taking it seriously even though we must've looked silly – grown men wrestling in skimpy trunks.

The next round got slippier, with more baby oil squirted in. The lads on the perimeter waiting their turn sprayed oil on the two battling it out in the pool.

Round three was similar, but this time with food stuff chucked in – tomato sauce and mayo. We were a sweaty, multi-coloured mess by the end.

For the final round, Chris set a challenge. We all got in, the goal being to yank each other's swimwear

CHAPTER TWELVE

off. The last one with trunks on wins. Any nerves were gone, and we dived in. It was like X-rated Twister, bodies contorted. One hand holding our own trunks on for dear life, the other trying to yank someone else's off. It was a slippery mess of muscles, bare bums, and willies flopping about! We were all just having fun. It was such a laugh and difficult to take too seriously. All the time though, I was focused on what the audience wanted and making sure I delivered.

I discovered naked wrestling was a boundary I was okay with. Erotic fun without being too sexual.

Chapter Thirteen

"PRIDE"

―

Bailey and I had become firm friends. Sidney too, though he was always off on his travels, leaving us to our own devices in London.

I'd managed to escape the hostel life, renting a single room in a shared house in East London. It wasn't perfect – the communal areas were a constant mess, and bringing girls back was a challenge with the paper-thin walls. But hey, it was a step up from hostels, sharing rooms with bunk beds and snoring strangers.

Adult work was good but sporadic, so I juggled it with cash-in-hand labouring jobs. I was the typical 'Jack of all trades, master of none', good at many things but lacked formal qualifications and training. That meant the worst jobs were always mine.

Demolition, for instance, was brutal. All day, I'd haul heavy rubble, filling wheelbarrows and

CHAPTER THIRTEEN

navigating treacherous stairs, the dust stinging my eyes and the noise pounding in my ears. The air hung heavy with the smell of concrete and sweat. It was exhausting, the £5 an hour barely enough to survive on. The extra cash from adult work was a lifesaver, but it couldn't be relied upon.

Then Nick from EnglishLads asked me to be a 'brand ambassador' at Brighton Pride. It was paid work. I said yes without hesitation, ADHD brain in full swing, not even knowing what it entailed.

On the day, we met at a bar in the heart of Brighton, a quiet before the storm. We stripped to the waist, and got EnglishLads painted across our muscular chests, flyers at the ready to promote EnglishLads.

I had zero Pride experience. Nothing could've prepared me for the explosion of joy that awaited.

The streets, once empty, now pulsed with life. A sea of rainbow flags, glitter, and outrageous costumes filled my vision. The air throbbed with music, laughter, and the rhythmic chants of marchers: "We're here, we're queer and we're not going shopping!" was one particular chant that made me smile.

The sweet scent of candyfloss mingled with the dark aroma of beer, adding to the intoxicating atmosphere. The sheer happiness was infectious.

The crowd was a kaleidoscope of ages, from toddlers in pushchairs to one remarkable woman who confided she was 87 and had only recently 'come out'. "Better late than never," I told her with a grin, genuinely moved by her courage. She beamed back, arm-in-arm with her "toy-girl", a sprightly 73-year-old. Witnessing their love and carefree, no fucks given attitude, filled me with a sense of hope.

It was at Pride I got my first real bear hug. I thought I knew what one was but this was different. It was from an actual bear! Ok, not the grizzly type but I was learning new terms to describe different gay men and discovered that a bear was a larger guy, often with a beard and a big hairy chest. To be fair, he did ask for consent and when I nodded my approval, suddenly, I was enveloped in a bear hug, feet lifted off the ground. A literal bear of a man, beaming with pride, he had recognised me from EnglishLads.

So many people did, and many wanted something from me. The requests included selfies, hugs and pecks on the cheek. My bum was tender the next day from being squeezed so often! Everyone was actually super respectful, and I didn't mind at all.

It was more than just the attention. All my life, I'd been labelled, judged, dismissed. Here, I was desired, seen as someone of value. The LGBTQ community embraced me, and for the first time, I felt like I belonged.

Often I felt invisible on the streets of Dublin as nobody made eye contact with the scruffy, smelly

CHAPTER THIRTEEN

kid. At Pride that day I felt wanted. People looked up to me like I was someone, when all my life I'd been a nobody. I had found my tribe, or more to the point they found me, and they have supported me from that day onwards and I bloody love them for it.

My connection with my fans, especially my gay ones, is genuine, built on mutual respect and appreciation.

Having been labelled by others all my life, I hate putting labels on myself. Personally, I think 'labelling' someone based on their sexuality is pointless. Especially when in most cases, the type of humans people are sexually attracted to is the least interesting thing about them.

I don't class myself as Gay or Bisexual. I'm sexually and romantically attracted to females. But I understand that the sexual interaction I have with both guys and women in my adult work confuses people. As far as I'm concerned when people ask me to label who I am, I just say 'I'm Andy', and that's enough. Labels are for clothes, not humans.

Sure, Pride was a bit overwhelming at first. The sights, the sounds, the open expressions of different sexualities were new to me. But I loved it. The attention fuelled me, and I thrived on entertaining my audience. Call me an attention-seeking whore if you like, I'll wear that label with pride.

SMELLY KID

The LGBTQ community embraced me, and for the first time, I felt like I belonged. It almost feels like I've been adopted by my gay fans, their loyalty consistent since those early EnglishLads days. I don't think most people grasp how meaningful it is for me to finally feel like I belong somewhere.

Being active on social media, though, inevitably invites trolls. Most of it I can brush off. A wise person once told me, "Don't accept criticism from someone you wouldn't take advice from," and that's stuck with me. But the accusation of 'gay baiting' stings. It's a murky term and different people say it means different things, but to me, it means straight performers teasing a potential gay audience with promises they don't keep. Flashing a bulge, hinting at male intimacy, but never delivering.

I've never done that. Not intentionally, anyway. My social media is upfront, and I give generous previews of my work. If anything, I over-deliver. That accusation hurts because it undermines the genuine connection I have with my audience. These are fans I truly love and value, and I'd never dream of misleading them or taking loyalty for granted.

That day, amidst the rainbow chaos, I met Ella. She was with a group of girls, curious about us EnglishLads boys. When she asked if I was gay, and I said no, she challenged me to prove it. I asked for a kiss, and then she realised I was serious. We swapped

CHAPTER THIRTEEN

numbers, a spark ignited amidst the Pride festivities.

A few days later, on a dusty building site, her text lit up my phone: "You're fit." It took a few exchanges to remember who she was as I'd met so many people at Pride.

We arranged a cinema date – my happy place. It was only recently that I connected my obsession with watching films on the big screen to my ADHD. Let me explain.

The very nature of the cinema means there are reduced distractions: The dark, enclosed environment minimises external stimulation, making it easier to focus on the film.

The large screen and surround sound create an atmosphere that helps hold my attention.

The set time and location provide a clear start and end, which can be helpful for people like me, with ADHD who sometimes struggle with starting or completing tasks.

It's social! Going to the cinema can be a shared experience with friends or family, giving connection and reducing feelings I get of isolation.

Finally, there is limited control. Unlike at home, you can't pause or rewind the movie, which encourages me to stay present and engaged.

It's odd though. I can thoroughly enjoy a movie and truly absorb it all. But don't bother asking me to explain the plot in detail afterwards!

Ella was different from me. Older, mature, with a responsible job and her own house. I felt a pang of inadequacy, unsure if we were a good match. After the film, we parted ways, and I couldn't shake the feeling that I'd blown it.

But then, she surprised me. She wanted another date. This time, we ended up back at her place. And, in typical ADHD fashion, I didn't just visit – I practically moved in. One minute I was feeling out of my depth; the next, I was fully immersed in a new relationship, my belongings scattered across her living room ready to start my next chapter as a proper grown up!

***

My first head shot

Photo from Crete holiday with Paddywack

Day out fishing with my local community centre

Don't ask

Me and Tintin (Michael)

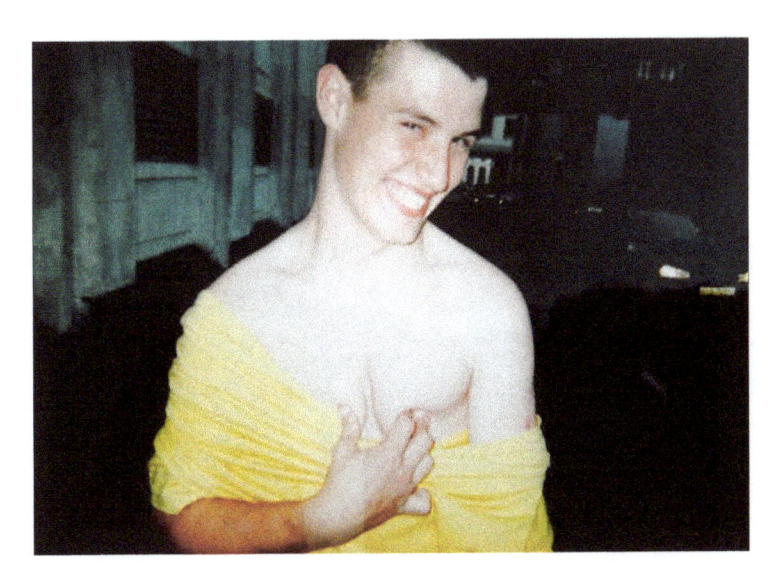

The only photo I have of Clayton

Me and Tintin on my 18th birthday

The beginning of my fitness journey

No longer a smelly kid

Bailey, me and Sidney, on the way to the pub on the day of Bailey's big revelation

Sidney and I on my wedding day

Me and my two best men Tintin, Bailey

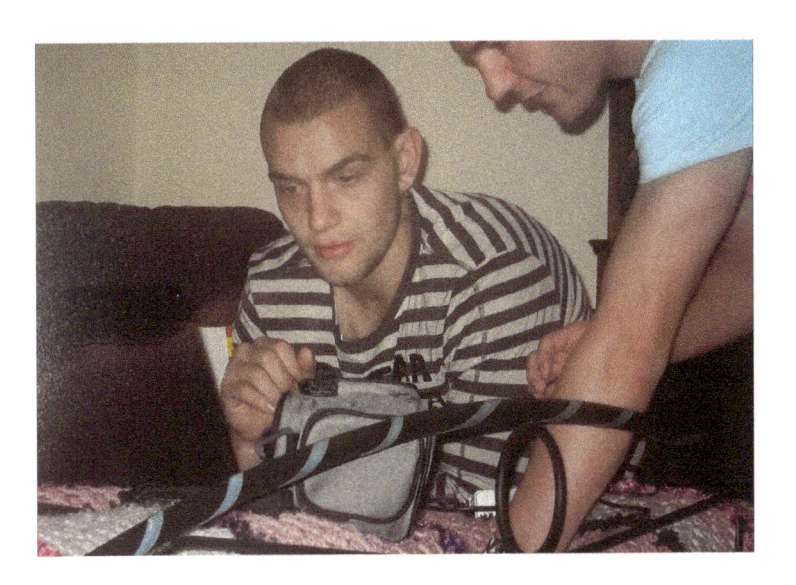

Booking my flight from Australia to London

Entertaining girlfriend Emma in Australia

Posing at Emma's piano

Me and Bailey at Brighton pride 2010 promoting EnglishLads

In Aberdeen hotel on the morning of my interview to work offshore

On set for Straight Lads Spanked

Me celebrating getting my dream bike with Sammie

My first day going offshore, wearing my survival suit

Excited to arrive on the oil rig for the first time

Proud moment working offshore

Proud moment working offshore

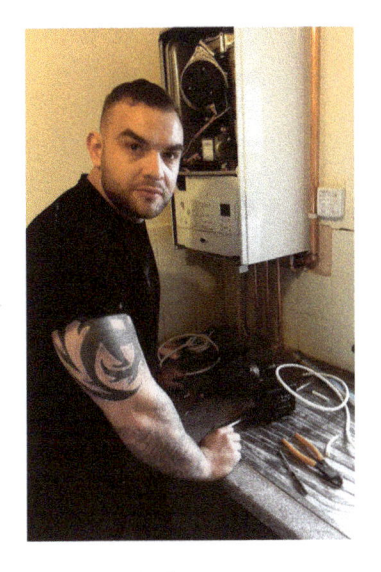

Andy the Gas man

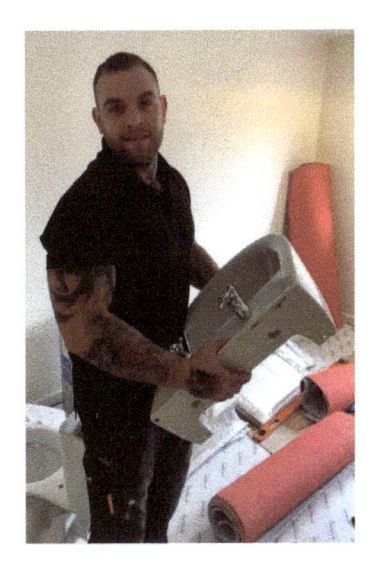

Installing a bathroom

The day I lost my dream job

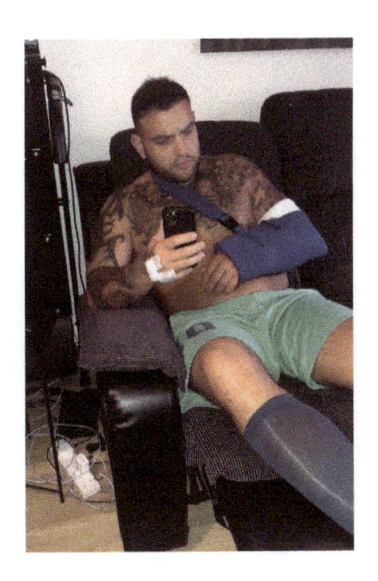

Depressed, injured and jobless

Me and Tintin, best friends forever

Chapter Fourteen

"JASON"

—

"Hello Andy, it's Jason, your dad."

The words hit me like a ton of bricks. It was 6 am in the morning, and I was barely awake, the morning light creeping into the home I was sharing with Ella in Slough. This phone call, something I'd thought about for most of my life, had come out of the blue. Here I was, 22 years old and I could barely speak, my voice all croaky from sleep and a jumble of feelings I wasn't ready for.

"Hi," I mumbled, my heart racing.

This was Jason, the man I'd only ever heard whispers about. The man my mum had met on the Isle of Man back in 1987, the man who was my dad.

Just the night before, Ella, who was now officially my girlfriend, had jokingly suggested I try finding my dad online. I'd laughed it off, thinking it was a waste of time. But her words stuck with me. With a mix of nerves and hope, I started searching for any sign of him.

It was tough going. Changed names, dead ends, nothing seemed to lead anywhere. Then I remembered something Mum had told me – Jason's brother, Duncan, was in a band called 'Mournblade'. I found the band, which led me to discovering my uncle's full name. On Facebook, I then messaged many people with that name, asking if they had a brother called Jason, but kept on hitting dead ends. Finally, one did reply and jokingly said, "Yes, I have a brother called Jason, does he owe you money or something?"

I said no, and we exchanged a few more brief messages, both of us being a little cagey.

Duncan suddenly said, "Are you Jason's long-lost son?"

"I think so," I replied nervously.

"Well, nice to meet you, Andy. I met your Mum, Louise!"

It was such a jolt to my system. Hearing Mum's name, I knew that I was speaking to my uncle. We chatted a bit more and Duncan shared more details about where Dad lived now and so on. At one point Duncan said to me cheekily, "Do you have the 'male' family trait?"

I immediately knew what he meant and laughed and said yes! I finally knew where I'd got my 'money

CHAPTER FOURTEEN

making' attribute from. We ended our chat, and Duncan gave me Jason's email address.

Ella, eager to support me, helped me compose a proper message to Jason, explaining who I was and that I wasn't looking for anything from him. We sent it late at night, not expecting to hear back anytime soon.

And now here he was, the very next morning on the other end of the line, his voice calm and steady. He told me his wife had opened the email and she was shocked. Jason had always known about me, but had decided not to tell his family, but he knew that one day I might reach out to him and he was ok with that.

He wanted to meet and we fixed a date and the next two weeks were filled with a mix of nervous excitement and anticipation. Every day felt like an eternity as I counted down the hours until I'd finally see him face-to-face. I replayed our brief phone conversation over and over, analysing every word he'd spoken. My mind raced with questions: What would he be like? Would he accept me? Would we have anything in common?

Two weeks later, he was there, standing before me in Slough. It felt surreal, like stepping into a different world. Jason was a world apart from the sun-drenched beaches of Australia and the wild nights in London. He was even further from the chaos and hardship I'd known growing up in Dublin.

Jason was everything I wasn't. He was calm, had his shit together, the picture of a normal life. He didn't drink, smoke, or do drugs. He was a roofer, a man who worked hard, building a life for himself and his family. He had two other kids, my brother and sister, and had given them the kind of stable life I could only have dreamt of.

As we talked, the full story came out. He'd met my mum when they were both just 18. Work was scarce in Ireland and Mum had travelled to the Isle of Man, taking on a seasonal job as a waitress in a restaurant. It was there she met Dad, a motorbike mechanic. They embarked on a summer romance that had unexpected consequences. After Mum returned to Dublin, she discovered she was pregnant. My grandmother, trying to do what she thought was right, had called Jason's mother to tell her about the pregnancy. Jason answered the phone, but was young and scared, and backed off from parental responsibilities. The phone call ending abruptly with nothing resolved.

And now, all these years later, here we were, my dad and I, dealing with what had happened that summer. I told him I didn't blame him at all for not wanting to be involved when he was just 18. Especially since Mum lived in a whole different country. I made it clear I wasn't here to cause any

CHAPTER FOURTEEN

problems for him, I just wanted to know where I came from. He listened, his eyes showing a hint of sadness and regret.

As we talked, the hours melted away. We shared stories, laughter echoing; he told me about his life in Somerset, his work, his family. I opened up about my own journey, the ups and downs, the losses and achievements. It was like two strangers, connected by blood, finally bridging the gap that had separated them for so long.

For the first time in my life, I felt a sense of fatherly connection, a thread tying me to something bigger than myself. We talked loads about my mum, her infectious laugh, her kind heart and how pretty she was. We talked about his family, his mum Sheila, his dad Brian, his brother Duncan – the very person who had connected us.

There was an ease between us, a natural flow of conversation that surprised me. It felt like we were picking up where we'd left off even though we'd never met. Two halves of a whole finally coming together.

As the afternoon drew to a close, a bittersweet feeling settled in. We'd shared so much, laughed and got to know each other, but the reality was, we had very, very separate lives. We said our goodbyes, and a hug made the day complete. I felt more warmth in that brief physical connection with my dad than

I'd ever felt from John. I watched Jason walk away, a sense of peace washing over me.

I didn't need a dad at that point in my life, and he didn't need any drama in his life. I was so glad I'd met him, glad I finally got to see the face of the man who'd given me life. It was like a piece of the puzzle clicking into place.

But for now, this chapter was over, a happy ending to a story that had started long before I was even born.

Yesterday I didn't have a dad; now today I did. Plus, a new brother and sister that I'd love to meet one day. From a lifetime used to the opposite happening, I welcomed this change and for once, felt positive and excited about the future.

✳✳✳

Chapter Fifteen

"OVER MY KNEE"

—

One day, desperate for cash, I was scouring job websites for any kind of work. A seemingly innocent Gumtree ad caught my eye, seeking "open-minded lads – next door types" for modelling work. The phrase "open-minded" hinted at something more adult-themed, so I sent a quick reply, attaching photos of Bailey and myself. I received a swift response; however, the details left me taken aback – unless I misunderstood, the job involved getting spanked for cash.

I was about to dismiss it as a dodgy waste of time, but something about the business-like tone of the email intrigued me. I called the number provided. The producer, calling himself "Mr X", explained he was working with Brett, a well-known model within the spanking world. I had no clue a spanking movie industry existed, let alone it having stars!

SMELLY KID

Honestly, I wouldn't have considered doing anything like this, but the producer made it sound easy, harmless, and fun. It really was just spanking, nothing sexual or intimate. Plus, the money was good, which I desperately needed. Mr X also seemed familiar with Bailey and me, knowing us from EnglishLads, and was eager to work with us both. I guess I was kinda flattered to be recognised, so I agreed, albeit reluctantly.

I told Bailey we had work that afternoon, but never actually explained what it involved and he never asked. I didn't fully understand it myself and would have struggled to describe it to anyone without it sounding bizarre. I figured we'd go along, see what it was about, and worst case, we'd leave. Mr X had already transferred our travel expenses, so we had nothing to lose but time.

We journeyed to East London, the directions leading us to a rough council estate filled with run-down looking flats. It was a stark contrast to the luxurious mansion where we filmed for EnglishLads and reminded me more of where I grew up in Dublin. I apologised to Bailey, thinking it was a mistake and suggested we head home. But after some discussion we decided we'd come this far, and might as well check it out. I still hadn't mentioned "spanking"!

We climbed the stairs to the fifth floor, hearts pounding, and nervously knocked on the peeling paint

CHAPTER FIFTEEN

of what we hoped was the correct door. Mr X greeted us warmly, ushering us into his living room, furniture stacked out of the way on one side, transforming it into a makeshift filming space. Brett, the supposed spanking world's Brad Pitt, was there, fiddling with a camera. He appeared moody and barely said hello.

"So, lads, have you ever been spanked before?" Mr X grinned.

"Spanked?" Bailey looked at me, a mixture of confusion and annoyance flashing across his face.

"Yes, spanked. Didn't Andy explain?"

I confessed I hadn't. An awkward silence followed, no one knowing quite what to say.

Finally, Mr X broke the tension, suggesting we start from scratch. He'd explain what was required, and we could decide if we wanted to participate. If not, no hard feelings, we could head home and he'd even give us cash for lunch. His reasonableness won us over, and I felt a pang of guilt for not being upfront with Bailey.

Mr X had created a "character" where naughty lads were sent to him for punishment. He pitched scenarios to us: football players sent by the coach, having received too many red cards, misbehaving apprentices sent by a frustrated supervisor. We settled on being builders sent by the boss for wolf-whistling at women, something Bailey and I might actually have done!

SMELLY KID

I asked Mr X why two burly lads would agree to get punished in his pretend world. He explained it was either that or get fired. It dawned on me that by asking this question I was seriously considering doing this. It actually sounded like a laugh.

Bailey seemed less enthusiastic. As he'd been given the option to leave with his expenses paid, I didn't feel too sorry for him. Once I commit to something, I give it my all. Mr X's genuine approach helped; I liked him. Brett, on the other hand, seemed stuck up and superior, which grated on me.

We got started. I'd never acted before, but playing a cheeky, misbehaving builder came naturally. The scene started with us handing Mr X an envelope from our fictional boss, containing a letter explaining our "crimes" and cash to pay Mr X for providing the "punishment". Mr X got into character, making it feel surprisingly real. After being lectured for a while about our 'made up', lecherous behaviour I soon believed I truly deserved a spanking!

Before long I found myself over Mr X's knee, pants down, Bailey grinning as my cheeks got slapped. It was surreal, me a 6ft 1 bruiser in this odd position, but once we got going, it was strangely fun.

Then it was Bailey's turn. He looked uncomfortable but, being competitive, didn't want to back down. I watched his peachy bottom turn red as he squirmed, trying to hide the pain, and I couldn't

CHAPTER FIFTEEN

help but laugh at how ridiculous it all was.

The filming didn't take long once we got started and we finished surprisingly quickly. It felt such a relief for it all to be over. As we were getting dressed, Mr X offered to double our pay if we filmed a second scene, this time spanking each other. We both instantly said no!

He suggested we think it over and left us alone to discuss it in private. I was tempted by the money, but Bailey needed convincing. "You better not spank me hard, or tell anyone else about this," he insisted. I reassured him I wouldn't.

Mr X invented a new scenario, keeping our same characters but this time we had been fighting at the building site. Mr X would explain that since we were so keen to hit each other, a suitable punishment would be the embarrassment of being ordered to spank each other. Again, little acting was needed; it was truly awkward and embarrassing. Weirdly, it felt easier being spanked by a stranger than it did being spanked by my mate. Bailey's discomfort amused me. Never did he imagine he'd be slapping my bare arse!

Despite how cringey it all was, we went ahead and filmed the scene. Ended up having a good laugh and got paid.

As we left with wallets bulging with cash, I thought that was it with regards to my spanking career. Little did I know I'd return to that flat more than 50 times, becoming good friends with Mr X.

A few days later, he called me. He and Brett had parted ways, Brett leaving him saddled with unpaid debts.

Mr X was only ever initially meant to be helping Brett behind the scenes. He had a regular job and wasn't hugely into the spanking stuff. However, he'd discovered a knack for producing these films, understood the niche and what the audience wanted, and in order to regain the money he'd lost through Brett, he decided to start his own website, "Straight Lads Spanked". He asked if I'd film more content with him immediately, and I jumped at the chance.

I have zero interest in the spanking fetish, but Mr X's passion for making good content was infectious. We always had fun, even though he was serious when it came to the filming, which I admired. He was also business-savvy and I definitely learned from him. Also, unlike my previous adult work, this wasn't sexual, just spanking. As long as I brought him new guys to film with, there seemed to be endless well-paid work for me.

One crazy memory stands out. I desperately wanted a specific motorbike but couldn't afford it. Mr X was out of filming ideas for me, so couldn't help. I had run out of mates to convince to film with me too. I was panicking as the bike owner had agreed to reserve it for me for 48 hours. I was determined to

CHAPTER FIFTEEN

get the funds no matter what. I had the idea to read the comments that had been left on the Straight Lads Spanked website. Some subscribers had requested a scene using stinging nettles as a spanking implement. Ouch! Another suggestion was using a wooden bath brush. Double ouch! I called Mr X, offering to do both if he paid enough for the bike. He agreed, emphasising it had to be done "properly" and it wasn't going to be easy. He joked I might not be able to sit on my bike to drive it home! I didn't care. I wanted that motorbike.

The next day, in a forest, I got my bare arse whipped with nettles. It was excruciating! Thankfully, Mr X had brought some soothing cream to take some of the heat out of my stinging cheeks once we were done.

We then went straight to his flat and filmed another scene using this wooden bath brush. It was brutal, leaving me with a bruised bum and real tears. But Mr X was thrilled with the content, and I got my bike.

He was right, though. I could barely sit for days. Still, totally worth it!

If that wasn't crazy enough, Mr X had this idea to collaborate with another spanking-themed studio based in Germany. The storyline was that my character's behaviour was so bad, I had to be taken to someone else to be dealt with. This guy, Steven, happened to be based in Germany. What it meant though was an all-expenses paid trip for Ella and I to go to Frankfurt! Mr X ended up shooting footage of me getting dragged by my ear, all the way from London, to the airport, on the plane and finally arriving in Germany. It was all so silly but absolutely hilarious! It was great publicity for Straight Lads Spanked, and again, I learned a lot from Mr X about the importance of promotion and getting people talking. Ella must have wondered what on earth she had got herself involved with as we filmed footage of me getting pulled by the ear onto an aeroplane!

Mr X ceased production of the movies many years ago now and is no longer involved in the industry. We still remain friends though to this day.

Filming those spanking scenes was a wild experience, pushing my boundaries in ways I never imagined. It was awkward and sometimes painful, but also hilarious. I embraced the absurdity of it all, focusing on delivering what the audience wanted while staying true to myself. Mr X's professionalism and support made it easier to navigate this new territory, and the financial rewards were undeniable. It was a far cry from the struggles of my past, and I was grateful for the opportunity to build a better life for myself and Ella, one spank at a time.

***

Chapter Sixteen

"ELLA"

Often when I get an idea in my head, it becomes all-consuming. It's hard to explain properly, but when I say all-consuming I really do mean that. I can't think of anything else. I'm usually unable to sleep or focus on any other task. Simple things like eating or brushing my teeth get forgotten about. Sometimes I feel like this is my superpower, as I end up doing things that everyone else thinks are crazy. Most of the time they are right. But occasionally I end up proving everyone else wrong and achieve something really special.

Ella and I had barely known each other a few weeks when the idea struck. Not just any idea, mind you, but the kind that grabs your ADHD brain by the scruff of its neck and screams, "DO IT NOW!"

We were on our way to Notting Hill Carnival, the streets buzzing with energy, the air thick with the scent of jerk chicken and the sounds of steel drums. And there, right in a jewellery shop window, was a ring. It wasn't flashy or expensive, but it was perfect. It just felt right.

Ella was great for me. She was stable, very mature, and made my life feel complete. We even had a little dog, Sammy, by this stage. So, with zero hesitation and a whole lot of impulsivity, I sneaked into the shop and bought that ring.

Fast forward to later that night. We're sitting at the bus stop, exhausted but buzzing from the carnival atmosphere. And that's when I did it. I whipped out the ring, looked Ella in the eyes, and blurted out, "Will you marry me?"

She looked at me, a mix of surprise and amusement dancing in her eyes. "Yes," she said, a smile spreading across her face. "Okay, let's do it, but don't tell anybody just yet."

Her parents weren't thrilled when we finally broke the news. Understandable, really. We'd known each other barely a month, and here we were, planning a wedding. But hey, when you know, you know, right?

Fast forward a few more months. We were actually getting married. My family flew over from Ireland – Auntie Linda, Auntie Teresa, my brothers' adopted parents, Ann and Tony, even a couple of my brothers. And Bailey, my best mate and partner in crime, was my best man.

CHAPTER SIXTEEN

The wedding day was a whirlwind; 150 guests on Ella's side, 15 on mine. It was the first time I'd seen my family in ages, and it was a blast introducing them to Bailey.

The whole day was full of laughs. At one point, a group came up to me, giggling. "We met your brothers outside," they said.

"How did you know they were my brothers?" I asked, confused.

"Because they were throwing stones at our cars!" they replied, cracking up. Apparently, some guests had been entertaining themselves by giving my brothers Red Bull and watching them go wild. Typical!

The day flew by in a blur of happiness and chaos. Ella and I were officially married.

We stayed married for about three years. We had some great times; however, we eventually realised we wanted different things out of life and discovered we were better as friends than as a couple.

So, we called it quits. It was amicable, a mutual decision and we are still in contact to this day. When I met Bailey, he was just visiting the UK and he later decided he wanted to continue his travels and ended up moving to Bali, and I haven't seen him since.

✳✳✳

Chapter Seventeen

"BULLIED"

I had very limited knowledge of oil rigs. I knew roughly what one looked like and understood that their purpose was to extract gas and oil from the seabed. But that was about it. Dave, a guy I cleaned windows for, worked on an oil rig, and I was quite envious of his lifestyle. It just seemed very exciting!

By this stage, I had worked for every UK-based adult website that would have me and even though I still got occasional offers of filming work, I nevertheless needed a regular job to pay the bills.

I had found myself back cleaning windows. It was very low pay, but the work was steady. I had two different scenarios where I cleaned windows. One of them was doing private houses, and I cleaned Dave's home. The other job was industrial cleaning, mainly hotels. I discovered when I worked in the hotels, I

CHAPTER SEVENTEEN

could get away with not doing much cleaning at all and instead catch up on my sleep!

Let me explain. At this time, I was back living in shared accommodation, renting a room in a busy house. There was always noise and late-night parties. I didn't usually participate in the fun, but it made it difficult to get a good night's sleep. So, I was back to being tired again, just like when I was little.

I had the job of cleaning the inside of the windows at these posh hotels. I'd arrive early in the morning, and reception would provide me with a list of all the unoccupied rooms and give me a master key for access. I discovered that the inside of the windows really weren't that dirty, and nobody bothered checking on my work. Those lovely big beds looked so inviting, and I just couldn't resist taking a nap. When I say a "nap", I could actually end up fast asleep for the entire morning. Nobody ever disturbed me, and I got away with this loads of times. I'd then just set my alarm for when I was due to finish, emerge from my room, hand my key back to reception, and leave! It was the easiest job ever!

Cleaning the windows of private homes was different; I actually had to do some work. I never minded that though, as I enjoyed making people happy and providing a good service. Dave and I just seemed to have become good mates. I was always asking him questions about his job on the oil rig and what it involved. He was a "Chief Steward".

A chief steward on an oil rig is like a hotel manager. They manage the team of stewards who ensure the living areas are always clean and comfortable for the crew. This includes everything from cleaning the cabins and communal living areas to helping the chefs prepare the meals and washing the dirty plates after mealtimes.

Dave explained how much a steward got paid, and it was a lot! They also usually only worked for half the year, often away for two weeks, then home for two weeks.

I thought this sounded like a brilliant job to have. The whole idea of working on an oil rig sounded thrilling! Especially the flying out by helicopter part. My ADHD brain kicked into gear, and I became obsessed. I wanted a job as a steward on an oil rig! Every time I saw Dave, I badgered him for more information. One day, I plucked up the courage and boldly asked him how I could get a job there. He explained it was so hard to get a placement if you didn't know someone. I cheekily pointed out that I did know someone. My mate Dave was a chief steward!

When he realised I was deadly serious, he said he would make some inquiries. A few days later, he came back to me and explained that he had spoken to the company he worked for, and they had agreed to

CHAPTER SEVENTEEN

give me an interview. The only problem was that, in order to even get an interview, you first of all had to participate in some offshore safety training, including sea survival and fire awareness. These all cost money. A lot of money. Not just the cost of the training but you had to travel to the training centres in Aberdeen and stay in hotels. I was just honest and explained I didn't have access to that kind of money. I was pretty much living hand to mouth at the time. I still don't fully understand exactly why to this day, but Dave then made me an incredible offer. He told me if I got £500 together, he would cover the rest. On the very strict understanding that once I was employed, I'd pay him back. It took me a week of grafting to get that money. I can't quite remember everything I did, but I got it. One thing I do remember was that I did a "private meet" job. I'd been made so many offers previously to do this, but always declined. It was just a bit out of my comfort zone. However, one guy made a very generous offer to pay me a substantial amount of money to watch me jerk off in person. That was it. Nothing more. No physical contact. I met him in a posh hotel. I was feeling so nervous as I waited for him in the lobby, I really thought I might be sick. However, the roles soon switched as we got into the lift – I realised he was trembling! I think he was both terrified and excited in equal measure. As we entered his suite, I was the one that calmed him down and suggested he take some deep breaths as I thought he was going to faint! Once he was more settled, I made myself relaxed on the bed and took care of business whilst he sat on a chair and just watched. The whole experience was over in about twenty minutes. I finished, got paid, and left.

I went back to Dave with the cash, and that seemed to prove to him that I was deadly serious. Before I knew it, I was up in Aberdeen, in a training centre, getting plunged into a swimming pool in this fake helicopter. They were simulating a crash landing into the ocean, and we were strapped into these seats, wearing bulky survival suits. As the helicopter went underwater, they flipped it upside down, and we had to undo our seat belts, push the window out of its frame, exit the helicopter, and swim to the surface! I felt like James Bond! It was terrifying and thrilling!

It took a few weeks in total to complete all the training, and true to his word, Dave got me an interview. This interview was like nothing I had done before. Everything was so professional, and it felt like there was so much at stake. Dave said I should wear a suit. I was so embarrassed as I didn't actually own one. The only time I'd ever worn one was when I was 12 at my mum's funeral. I used what little cash I had left and rushed to Primark, where I managed to get a complete suit that nearly fitted for £40. I borrowed shoes and a tie off one of my

CHAPTER SEVENTEEN

housemates. I had prepared a CV, my first ever. Dear readers, I'll be honest, I had to be creative to make my employment history look consistent. I really felt like a fraud and I was terrified of being exposed for being the smelly, good-for-nothing, toe-rag from Dublin. What was a loser like me doing even expecting to be taken seriously by what seemed like the very clever people who were interviewing me? The interrogation began, and I was feeling so out of my depth. I was being asked about previous experience working in kitchens and cleaning hotel rooms, and I was struggling to answer properly. I could tell it was all going badly wrong as I was stuttering and fumbling my way through their questions. Eventually, my ADHD brain kicked in, and I suddenly blurted out, "Look, I know I don't have all the work experience you want me to have. I could sit here and make it all up and pretend to be something I'm not, but I'm not going to do that. Instead, all I can do is simply beg you to give me a chance. I'm a quick learner, and I'll do whatever I'm asked to do and if I don't know how to do it, I'll only need to be shown once. I'm certain that out of everyone you are interviewing today, I'm the least qualified and experienced for this job. But I also know that I want this more than anybody else. I just need this break and if you give me a chance, I won't let you down."

SMELLY KID

They seemed very taken aback and a bit uncomfortable. I was told they'd be in touch either way.

I left feeling deflated. Convinced I'd messed up, and had no idea how I was going to pay Dave back. The train back to London felt like the longest journey ever.

The very next morning, my phone rang. It was a withheld number.

"Is that Andy?" the lady with the strong Scottish accent asked.

"Yes," I replied.

"I'm delighted to tell you that we would love to have you working for us. When can you start?"

Two weeks later I found myself flying to Aberdeen with Dave. I had been allocated to work with him for my first trip! He was going to be my boss. I was so excited!

Dave knew all about my adult work and he strongly suggested that I treat the oil rigs as a brand new chapter in my life and to not mention to the other guys I'd be working with that I was a porn star. He quite rightly said I should let people judge me for who I am, not what I'd done. It all made sense and I agreed with him.

We checked in at the heliport at Aberdeen, sat through a flight safety briefing, and were allocated our sea survival suits and life jackets. The wait for

CHAPTER SEVENTEEN

the helicopter seemed to last forever. I noticed that hardly any of the guys spoke to each other and they all seemed quite sad, which I didn't understand as I was just buzzing with excitement. However, Dave explained that most of them had just said goodbye to their families, knowing they wouldn't be seeing them for several weeks, which I understood.

Soon enough, we were called to board. It was a long walk to the helicopter that already had its engines fired up and was roaring away! I struggled to fasten my seatbelt but one of the other guys helped me, which I appreciated, and then we were off! I loved travelling by helicopter; there were more twists and turns than a regular plane, and it was exhilarating. I was sitting there, wide-eyed and absorbing it all, while most of the other guys were snoring!

We soon landed and had to duck when leaving the chopper as the blades were still spinning and I didn't want to lose my head. The helipad on the oil rig was so high up, and the stairs we had to take were just metal grids with the rough ocean visible hundreds of feet below us. We entered the main platform through this thick heavy door, and as soon as it was closed, everything was deadly quiet. It was like entering a different world. A very efficient world where everything had a place and a time. There was a rule for everything, from what time you ate to where you put your dirty clothes to be laundered, to when you could access the internet after work. I got allocated my cabin but couldn't enter as my roommate was on nights and was fast asleep. We all did a 12-hour shift. Day shift was 0700 till 1900 and nights were the opposite. So I barely met my cabin mate as he started work when I finished. He was on the top bunk and I had the bottom.

Dave showed me through to the recreation room and introduced me to the other stewards, my new workmates, who were on a tea break. Dave then had other stuff to do and just left me to get settled in and have some tea and cake. This cake was baked fresh on the oil rig by the night baker and tasted so good. There seemed to be an endless supply of snacks which I took advantage of.

Everyone was just making small talk and seemed very friendly. One of the lads asked me where I'd worked before as he thought he recognised me, and before I knew it, my mouth had opened and I was saying, "I've mainly been doing porn work but I don't think you recognise me for that". As I was saying those words, my brain was saying "shut up, Andy, shut up", I knew I'd fucked up. It honestly felt like it was someone else speaking. I hadn't planned to say anything at all and here I was, less than an hour on the platform, speaking to a bunch of burly oil rig workers about my work getting my dick out to entertain a gay audience. Nobody could quite believe

CHAPTER SEVENTEEN

what I was saying so I found myself getting my phone out to show some publicity photos I had! It was at this moment that Dave walked back into the room and I quickly shoved my phone back in my pocket as everyone went quiet. Dave could tell something was going on and found a way to get me on my own.

"Andy, please don't tell me that you told them about porn?" he pleaded.

"Erm, it might have accidentally slipped out, I'm so sorry, Dave, I honestly didn't mean to!"

I'll never forget his look of utter disbelief and disappointment. I really did feel terrible.

As it happens, at the time of writing this book, Dave probably understands my crazy ADHD brain more than anyone else. I run all my mad ideas by him, and he is the only person that can tell me I shouldn't do something and I'll listen to him. If I'm worked up by something, I can call Dave and he always knows how to bring me back down to a place of calm. He totally gets me. Back then though, he was just getting to grips with the full extent of my weirdness and I can't imagine how he must have felt.

"Well, what's done is done," he said. "Fuck it, you have done nothing wrong and you shouldn't have to hide who you are." His words were reassuring to me.

I really enjoyed my first trip offshore. The lads I worked with were great fun and I actually quite enjoyed the work. I learned a lot of new skills, from working in the laundry, operating the industrial washing machines and driers, to how to polish the dining room floor! Yes, I was known as the 'gay porn guy' but nobody dared to say anything bad about it to my face. I actually don't think anyone really cared. They just thought I was 'off my head' which is true!

My next trip offshore didn't go so well. Dave wasn't out with me this time and there was a different Chef Manager on than my time before. The Chef Manager, even though they work alongside the chief steward, is overall in charge of the entire catering team, so that's all the chefs and the stewards. Usually, the chef manager concentrates on the kitchen, or galley as it's called on the rig, and leaves the stewards to the chief steward to manage. The Chef Manager I had on my first trip was a brilliant guy called Robert. I really respected him. He pretty much left me alone but always checked in on me to make sure I was ok. This new guy, Scott, was totally different. He was ex-army and still acted like he was in the military. He clearly had it in for me from day one. I think he thought that because I was mates with Dave, he had to make an extra effort to show everyone that I wasn't getting special treatment. So, he treated me like shit! I also think there was an element of homophobia going on. You see Dave was gay, though most people wouldn't know unless he told them. He didn't make a big deal about it,

CHAPTER SEVENTEEN

but he had worked on oil rigs for a while and many people knew. Nobody cared. Everyone liked Dave. He was a good boss. However, Scott, I think, was making some connection (that didn't exist) between me having done gay porn and my friendship with Dave. I think Scott had always had an issue with Dave being gay, but couldn't express it, and now he had an opportunity and took it out on me.

Everything I did wasn't good enough. He spoke to me like I was a useless piece of shit. Everyone else noticed it. I just didn't have the skills to handle it. So I just went quiet. I really tried hard to please Scott, but it was impossible. One time he put on a pair of white gloves and wiped a finger on a floor I'd just mopped to see if I'd cleaned it properly. It was ridiculous.

I ended that trip and went home feeling deflated. My next trip was great again as Robert was back in charge and all he did was encourage and praise me.

My third trip, Scott was back on, and it went from bad to worse. Dave actually flew out to start his shift a week after I'd been there. It was the first time we had worked together when Scott was present.

I hadn't seen Dave for a while, and once he got settled in, he found where I was working and came to say hello. I wasn't being singled out; Dave went to say hello throughout the day to all the stewards. We had only been chatting for about a minute when Scott suddenly appeared from the shadows and said, "you lover boys can have your romantic reunion when the shift is over". Dave was clearly flustered and left with Scott. I was left absolutely raging. I was angry at how he had spoken to me but even more pissed off that Dave was being affected too. I felt really responsible for it all, even though I'd done nothing wrong.

I don't know what Dave said to Scott, he didn't tell me, but I know he wouldn't take any shit.

One of the lads had a load of DVDs for sale. Boxsets of TV shows. I ended up buying some, and Dave and I would often watch them in my cabin after work. This was not unusual. All the guys did this. We were always in and out of each other's cabins. We watched this amazing TV show called The Returned. It was in French with English subtitles. I'd never watched anything with subtitles before and felt so sophisticated. We both got hooked on this spooky show and were excited to finish work to watch the next episodes. However, it got back to Scott that Dave had been in my cabin and the next day he was making all kinds of inappropriate gay slurs to me. It was horrible. It was so stupid as other guys had also been in and out of my cabin but nothing was said.

I wish I could go back in time and deal with it differently. Nowadays, I'd never allow anyone to bully me or any of my friends. Back then, I just didn't know how to handle it and mainly kept quiet.

CHAPTER SEVENTEEN

I lasted about 18 months working on the oil rigs before calling it a day. I can't say Scott's bullying was the only reason I left, but he was a huge part of my decision. Also, I'd just got a bit bored of the work and my ADHD brain was telling me to find some new challenges. So, I handed in my notice.

I'd love to say that the last thing I did was give Scott the slap he deserved, but I didn't do or say anything to him. I think I was conscious of not making things harder for Dave who still had to work there. I did vow though that I'd never allow anyone to ever speak to me like that again, and I never have.

I'm forever grateful to Dave for giving me that opportunity. He saw something in me that nobody else had. One of my proudest achievements was getting my first pay from the oil rig and within minutes, I'd transferred everything I owed back to him. I'm aware I have many faults, but one thing I am is fiercely loyal to those who have my back and Dave still does to this day. I don't really know how to describe what we have, but I'm so glad to call him my mate. Scott, however, can go fuck himself.

✳✳✳

Chapter Eighteen

"CAN'T ESCAPE THE PAST"

I'd learned from my time working on oil rigs that it was the guys who had a proper trade that earned the most money. I was back to being unemployed again but this time it felt different. I was different. I had learned so much. Not just about the world of work but about who I was as a person. I knew that I had value and that I could bring value to others. I no longer believed that I was 'less than' other people.

I'd also experienced having money. Not just enough money to pay for a night in a hostel and get a value meal from the supermarket, but enough money to pay my rent in advance, run a car, have a decent phone and go on holidays. I was determined not to go backwards. I wasn't going to allow myself to be hungry again.

CHAPTER EIGHTEEN

I had managed to save a good chunk of money and had decided it was going to be used to invest in myself.

The very day after I returned home from my last trip working offshore, I happened to notice my local college had an open day. I'm certain they would have had them many times previously, but I'd have just walked by and not paid any attention. College wasn't for the likes of me!

This time I walked straight in and was met by a friendly guy who was handing out leaflets. "What trade pays the most money?" was my question when asked if he could help with anything. "Plumbing and Gas," he replied without hesitation. He pointed me towards the correct stand and before I knew it, I was in a different room sitting an aptitude test to check my basic maths and English skills. Despite my chaotic school life, I actually had an ok grasp of basic maths and arithmetic and even though I'm not much of a reader my understanding of written English has always been acceptable.

Well, I passed the tests easily and had it officially confirmed. I wasn't totally stupid!

That day I enrolled on a training course and my journey towards being a gas and heating engineer began! For years previously, in a lot of my adult work, I'd often been given the role of being a 'Tradie'. Now I was actually going to have my own trade.

It's in situations like this that my ADHD brain really is my superpower. If I really want something I can hyper focus on it to the point of obsession where nothing else matters. The next few years were a blur as I attended night classes and some weekends. I lived as much as I could off my savings but took as much freelance work as I could fit in. Mostly labouring. I fully immersed myself in the learning and took every advantage to fast-track my training as much as possible.

Once I qualified, I initially got a job working for a company servicing gas cookers in posh hotels in London. I then set up my own heating and plumbing business with a mate of mine. That was ok for a while, but I realised over time I was much better at this stuff when I had full control and didn't have to rely on others. This is not meant as a criticism of anyone else, but when my brain is fired up, I don't stop. If there is work to do, I'll get up super early and not stop that day until I can't work any more. It's unfair of me to expect that of others, so I realised I'm better off having sole control.

I continued working like this for several more years and built up a good reputation as being a reliable tradesman.

A friend of mine had a job working with the local council and gave me the heads up that a position had become available, heading up a team of gas engineers that were servicing various council-run estates.

CHAPTER EIGHTEEN

I doubted I would even be in with a chance as even though I had the qualifications necessary I still hadn't been doing it as long as many others.

Again though, I felt different. I had a new confidence that told me I was not only worthy of this position but that I was going to get it.

And I did! One thing I gained from Dublin is some cheeky Irish charm and I used that to its full potential during my interview.

This was such a step up for me. I no longer needed my tools as I was managing others. I was now a leader, check me out! The job had a lot of responsibility, but again, my ADHD brain seemed suited to the attention to detail that this managerial role required.

As time went on, I discovered that I loved this job so much. It paid well and I was good at it. I liked the team I worked with, and they seemed to respect me. I never took respect for granted. It meant nearly everything to me to be looked upon with approval rather than disgust.

One day, my boss, Stuart, summoned me for a meeting with a video call. I wasn't overly concerned; after all, things were going well. Little did I know, this seemingly ordinary meeting would turn my entire world upside down.

I'd been out getting food with my pal Kris, and I said I needed to go home to take a Zoom call; he agreed to come with me.

SMELLY KID

I joined the call from my home office. A strange sense of unease washed over me as I saw my boss's serious expression. He cleared his throat, his voice heavy with accusation. "I've come across something about you," he began, his voice sounding stern.

My heart pounded in my chest. I tried to remain calm, but a wave of panic washed over me. What could he possibly know? My mind raced, searching for any explanation.

Then, he dropped the bomb. "I've seen your adult work on Twitter."

The world seemed to stop. A cold dread settled over me. How could he have discovered my secret life? Not just my secret life but a life that was in the past.

My well-earned professional image as a contract manager shattered in an instant.

I went into defence mode. "What's it got to do you, this is my private life and nothing to do with my work?" I asked.

"It's got everything to do with me. I've seen the images of what you do with other guys and it's disgusting. You make me sick." He actually looked like he might be sick, he was that repulsed.

In that moment I realised I was once again a victim of homophobia. Which was slightly ridiculous as I'm not gay.

CHAPTER EIGHTEEN

Kris had no idea about my past work in gay porn. He was quite conservative in nature, and I'd never mentioned it. I'd learned my lesson from the oil rig about keeping that work separate from my regular life. But here was Kris, finding out in this clumsy way about my murky past as he was in full earshot of the conversation.

My boss and I went back and forward for about 15 minutes and got nowhere. He was adamant that I had brought the company into disrepute, and I knew that I hadn't. Nobody else at work knew about this other than my boss.

Even if it did get out at work, I hadn't done anything illegal and it was all in the past.

Eventually I asked Stuart, "What do you want to come out of this conversation?" And he said, "I want you to resign today." I told him I didn't want to resign today. This was my dream job. I told Stuart I had my heart set on being a project manager of a new build of council flats, and that was the direction my work was heading. There was so much further potential for me. He said, "No, I want you to resign today."

Stuart explained that if this went to a hearing he would use his influence to ensure I got fired. Alternatively, he gave me the option of resigning there and then and I would get three months' pay and would go on immediate gardening leave so I didn't have to do any further work. I told him I would need some time to think about this. I then got some legal advice and I was told that it was pointless for me trying to work in a company who no longer wanted me and because I hadn't been there for that long, they held all the power. I feel ashamed to say this now, but I called Stuart back and literally begged him to let me keep my job. I told him that my adult work was all in the past and it was never going to happen again, but that I was powerless to remove old content from the Internet. But he wasn't having any of it and again made it clear that I had to resign with immediate effect – so I did. The timing couldn't have been worse, we were right at the beginning of lockdown during Covid and there was no way I could get new work as a self-employed gas engineer. I had also torn a muscle in my bicep and was injured and couldn't train, and things suddenly started spiralling down on me: I had no income, no job, my physical health wasn't good due to my injury and I was putting on weight. I was potentially facing bankruptcy. I honestly didn't know what I was going to do. It felt like my life was over. Even though I didn't have serious suicidal thoughts I just kept on thinking over and over, what is the point of getting out of bed? Then I discovered OnlyFans and went on to discover that my life, rather than being finished, had barely even begun!

***

Chapter Nineteen

"ONLYFANS SAVED MY LIFE"

One day, I had my dream job, at which I excelled. The next day, it was abruptly taken away, leaving me with nothing. Losing important things seemed to be a constant theme in my life. This time, the loss hit harder than I can remember feeling before. It felt so unjust that one man's prejudice could have such a devastating impact on my life. For a while, I resented the adult industry, blaming it for my job loss. I now realise I was being unfair. I lost my job due to Stuart's homophobia. I'm certain that if the images he'd seen were of me getting raunchy with beautiful women, he would've been slapping me on the back, saying, "well done, lad!".

My bicep injury was also a major setback. The gym had been my sanctuary. I love training; it simply makes me feel good. It's a strange contradiction: it helps me burn off excess energy, calming my

ADHD brain, while also providing a natural high that motivates me. For a huge part of my life, I'd been such a weak, skinny kid that was easily bullied. Building muscle felt like armour around me.

My arm injury hindered my training, and I lost all motivation to go to the gym. So, I turned to food for comfort. It was false comfort, though. While I enjoyed the eating, I hated the way I looked as the weight piled on. Money was also becoming scarce.

Lockdown was a terrifying time. My ability to earn was drastically reduced. Even casual labour jobs were hard to find. My mental health was in a terrible state. I kept dwelling on my past adult work negatively, wishing I could erase it all from the internet.

But over time, my attitude softened. I reminded myself how much that work had been a lifesaver when I needed it. I also recalled the fun I'd had. Nearly all my filming experiences had been positive, and I'd always been treated respectfully. More importantly, I admitted to myself that I was good at making porn. I understood the audience and was skilled at delivering what they wanted. So, I gradually shifted my mindset. I thought, "Well, I've tried to leave this industry behind, but it hasn't worked. So, I might as well embrace it fully. Lockdown might have been bad for many businesses, but porn sites were booming as people were stuck, bored at home

CHAPTER NINETEEN

looking to be entertained."

I was certain about one thing: I never wanted to work for someone else again. I wouldn't give another employer the power to dismiss me on a whim. I applied this new approach to adult work. The days of getting a one-off fee while the website owner profited endlessly were over. I don't begrudge them for that, but I was a different person now, not the clueless kid who first worked for EnglishLads.

I initially focused on my Twitter account. I knew I had a fanbase scattered across the internet, that liked me for different things. Some from the erotic wrestling, others knew me from EnglishLads, and of course there were fans from the Straight Lads Spanked days. I wanted one central place for them all to find me, so I established AndyLeeXXX on Twitter. I posted what content I could, and my following grew rapidly. I soon had hundreds of thousands of followers.

Around this time, I discovered OnlyFans. It felt like perfect timing. I'd been vaguely aware of it before, but hadn't given it much thought. News reports of creators making incredible sums of money had gained my interest. I researched it and realised OnlyFans was the ideal platform for my relaunch.

This time, I'd be in full control of my content and keep most of the earnings. I was excited about directly connecting with my fans. I was tentatively back to training and getting back in shape, so the timing felt right. The only issue was lockdown restrictions.

I had a garage I rarely used and decided to turn it into a film studio. It was small and cramped, but I made it work. Initially, the quality was poor due to lack of proper equipment. I quickly learned the importance of good lighting. I invested in better lighting gear and improved my camera.

I realised I was limited by only doing solo performances. My subscribers deserved more. I needed to collaborate with others to spice things up. I understood the appeal of masculine, hetero guys pushing the boundaries of their sexuality for a gay audience, and that's what my subscribers wanted. This is how 'Team Andy' was born. I convinced some of my mates to join me in the garage, and I realised I'd taken on the role of producer.

With gyms reopening, I found a new place to recruit guys. My attitude towards porn work had completely changed. It was no longer a dirty secret. I openly discussed it with anyone who asked.

I surprised many guys. They never would've considered adult work, especially for a gay audience. But they saw me, a big, muscly, confident tattooed guy, openly talking about jerking off in my garage, and I made it sound as normal as working on a construction site. I wasn't shy about mentioning the

CHAPTER NINETEEN

good pay it brought either. Even in those early days I could sometimes earn more in a day than I did in a full week as a gas engineer. Guys would approach me discreetly, asking how to get involved. Soon, they were in my garage, work trousers down, wanking off beside me.

It had become normal for me, and my relaxed attitude gave others the confidence to join in. Plus, don't underestimate the competitive nature of some guys. If I could do it, they thought they could too. I recruited guys from all walks of life, even convincing an Uber driver to join me.

In the early days, I paid the guys for their work. Now, I usually work with other creators who rather than needing paid, they get the content we film for their own OnlyFans. I also help brand new guys get started with OnlyFans – but more about that later.

With relaxed lockdown rules, I had more opportunities to film in different locations. I'd use gym locker rooms after hours or rent Airbnbs and hotels. But as my OnlyFans grew, I needed a permanent filming space. My friends suggested I rent a small lock-up or empty shop, but I had bigger plans.

I found a huge, abandoned warehouse that was available to rent. It was a complete ruin inside and wasn't even connected to the power grid. Everyone thought I was crazy, but I saw its potential. The first weekend I had the place completely cleared of all the rubble and debris. There was a lot! I filled a large truck over ten times and become on first name terms with the staff at my local refuse centre. Next step was getting the electrics sorted. That was frustrating as I couldn't do that myself and had to rely on others and it seemed to take forever, but eventually we had power! I soon got to work building lots of different sets to film in. Ranging from a locker room, to a lad's bedroom, to an erotic sex dungeon! My studio had it all and I was pumped to take my content creation to a whole new level. What I hadn't anticipated was nearly getting arrested in France for filming a porno at the Eiffel Tower.

***

On set playing a police officer

Pornstar university main floor

Mechanic garage set

Builders set

Locker room set

Main floor set

Living room set

Bedroom set

Army barracks set

Classroom set

Hang out area

Ready for a day of erotic oil wrestling

Dr Andy Lee will see you now

On the way to Paris, discovered an oil leak in the taxi

Me, Daisy and Lacey at the Eiffel Tower

*Just about to measure myself for 'My massive C**k' in front of the nation*

Only Andy documentary cover photo

Me with Mark Hassell after winning my first Snap award for male performer of the year 2023

Red carpet at xbiz awards Amsterdam 2024

Beaming with joy after winning a Snap award for the second year running

My first time revisiting Dorset Street flats on the stairs where we use to play outside

Standing outside my home at Dorset Street flats

Revisiting Sunshine House

Me in New York

Dorset Street flats as they were being demolished

Drinking gold leaf coffee at Emirates Palace, Abu Dhabi

Dune bugging in the desert, Dubai

My first experience at Premiere cinema

Me and Ryan in New York

Dubai

Bangkok, Thailand

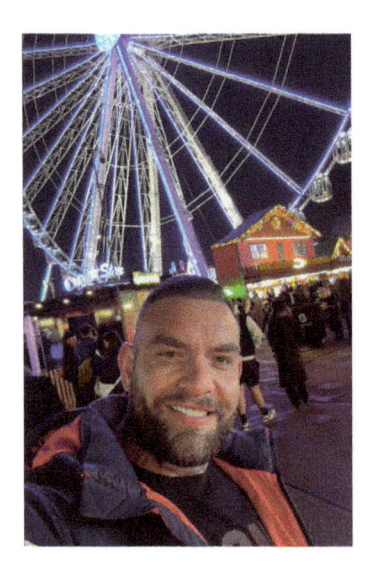

Winter wonderland, London

Taj Mahal, India

Celebrating my 36th birthday in a posh hotel, London

Chicago

A smelly kid travelling first class

Chapter Twenty

"EYEFUL TOWER"

"Dave, I'm going to buy a traditional London Black Taxi, drive it to Paris, and film a porno in front of the Eiffel Tower," I said excitedly.

"I'm sorry, I thought for a second I heard you say that you're going to buy a traditional London Black Taxi, drive it to Paris, and film a porno in front of the Eiffel Tower," Dave responded, sounding confused.

"Yeah, that's right. It's going to be epic," I said, super excited.

"Andy, are you actually okay?" Dave asked, sounding genuinely concerned.

"Yeah, I'm absolutely fine. Don't you think it's a great idea?" I asked him.

"Well, I'll be honest, I'm struggling to process it all. Let me ask you a few questions," Dave said, using the voice he uses when he thinks I've lost my mind. I hear this voice most days!

"Where will you get a taxi from?"

"I've no idea, but I'll get one."

"Are you even sure you can drive a taxi into France?"

"No idea, but I'll just do it."

"Who are you going to film this porno with?"

"No idea, haven't really thought that far."

"Okay, what's the actual point of it all?"

"I'm not really sure, to be honest, but it's going to be amazing."

"Have you maybe considered doing it in Blackpool instead?"

"Absolutely not. That's a crazy idea."

"But Paris isn't a crazy idea?"

"No, Paris is the place to do it."

"Have you been to France before?"

"Nope."

"Okay, well, I think you're out of your mind."

"Thanks, Dave, I knew you'd understand."

Dave was right, of course. I hadn't thought any of this through, but my ADHD brain wouldn't let me stop thinking about it. Over time, Dave kind of mellowed and agreed it would, at the very least, get people talking.

Well, I couldn't have predicted just how much it would get people talking. Here's what happened:

I found an old taxi for sale. Considering how many miles it had done, the bodywork still looked

CHAPTER TWENTY

good, which was all I really cared about.

Finding models to film with was trickier, as nobody else shared my enthusiasm for driving to France. However, I eventually persuaded two brilliant adult content creators, Lacey and Daisy, to accompany me on my continental road trip.

The trip to Dover was uneventful. My camera operator and the girls were in the back. I had to keep the speed low, as apparently, it wasn't very comfortable riding in the back of the cab, especially over bumps. In London, cars barely go over 20mph, so I guess the taxis weren't built for speed.

The ferry ride across the Channel was fun. They served good food, which I enjoyed. The waiter was very attentive, constantly checking if we needed anything. At one point, the girls disappeared to the bathroom, leaving me alone. The waiter approached me and nervously said, "I've been following you since EnglishLads. Any chance I can have a picture with you?" I could see he was all shy and possibly a bit star struck!

"Of course." I grinned. I love meeting fans. We took a selfie, he asked for a hug, and I obliged and he seemed very pleased. When we finished our meal, he told me the bill was taken care of. I insisted on paying, but he wouldn't have it. I thanked him and gave him another hug and as the shores of Calais became visible, we headed down to the car deck excited for what lay ahead.

SMELLY KID

We'd only been driving in France for about ten minutes when the oil warning light came on. I ignored it for a moment but stopped immediately when I saw smoke coming from the engine.

The knowledge I'd gained from helping my mate fix up his car years ago when I was homeless, proved useful. I identified an oil leak. This wasn't good. However, I wasn't going to let it stop me. Fortunately, there was a petrol station nearby, and I stocked up on oil. It was only a slow leak, and we managed to reach Paris, stopping every half hour or so to top up.

We eventually found the perfect parking spot. It wasn't as private as I'd hoped, but I'd tinted the windows of the taxi for some privacy.

I donned a cloth cap, which was my attempt at a cab driver costume, and the girls got dressed, or more accurately, undressed, into sexy short skirts: Lacey in knee-high boots and Daisy in heels. They looked amazing.

First, we took some risqué photos by the taxi, with the Eiffel Tower looming in the background. We recorded a bit of promo footage, with me asking the girls, "Where do you want to go, loves?"

"Just the Eiffel Tower," they responded.

"I'll give you the Eiffel Tower," I replied cheekily.

We got into the back of the taxi and started filming the saucy content. I'll spare you the explicit details; however, the windows steamed up pretty quickly.

CHAPTER TWENTY

Suddenly, there was a knock on the front window. I quickly pulled up my trousers and opened the door.

The sight of armed police was terrifying. They didn't look pleased. I tried to explain that we were professionals, and even though they were mainly speaking in French I heard the words 'disgusting' and 'criminal'. This had suddenly turned serious.

I had a vision of myself in French custody, calling Dave for help, and him saying, "I told you so". I wasn't going to let that happen!

Things calmed down, and I managed to convince them to let us go if I deleted the recordings. They agreed, on the condition that we return home immediately. I readily accepted and deleted the files.

We quickly drove away but had to stop in the middle of traffic to top up the oil. I thought we were going to be arrested again, but I was quick and got on our way.

I felt gutted that our trip was a waste, with no footage to show for it. Then I remembered I'd taken the early publicity shots on my phone, so all was not lost. The UK's leading tabloid, The Sun, loved the story and featured it with the headline, 'Eyeful Tower'!

It went viral and boosted the subscribers of my OnlyFans page. I learned the importance of getting people talking about me.

SMELLY KID

When I first told Dave about the Paris idea, I knew it was about publicity, but my brain couldn't explain it properly. Now I truly understood.

Speaking of going viral, little could I have imagined just how much the nation would be talking about me as I found myself, fully naked, on a prime-time documentary, featuring men with big cocks!

***

Chapter Twenty-One

"ONLYFAMS"

Over the years, I gradually got back in touch with my brothers and sister, who were all still living in Dublin. When I first left for Australia, we were scattered, living with different family members so we weren't that close, and most were too young for phones or social media.

Time passed, and things changed. We reconnected on Facebook, swapped numbers, and started chatting. After a few months in England, my brothers started visiting one by one. We were all broke, and they wondered about also making money in adult films. I didn't push them, but I couldn't stop them either. That's just how we are, headstrong and stubborn.

One of my brothers started working for English Lads, and a few others met Mr X from Straight Lads Spanked. I often tagged along, and sometimes we'd get paid extra to film together. It might sound weird, but growing up in a big family, with little privacy and sharing everything, we were pretty open.

As kids, we were used to sharing bedrooms, beds, and baths. So, jerking off together for good pay wasn't a big deal to us. It meant we could afford fun stuff like going to the cinema, eating out, or visiting a theme park.

Dear reader, you may have noticed that I've tried to focus on my own story, not others'. It's not about ego, but about respecting their experiences. My siblings went through a lot, and their stories are theirs to tell.

When I started OnlyFans, some brothers wanted in. It was a good deal for everyone. They could fly over from Dublin for work, then go back to normal life. No one would know unless they saw the videos, which was unlikely. By then, Patrick and Aoife were also living in England.

Out of the blue, a TV producer hit me up on Twitter, asking if I wanted to be in a TV show about having a big penis. They'd seen my stuff on AndyLeeXXX and thought I was perfect.

I was intrigued. A week later, we met for coffee. The show, "Too Large For Love", would explore the challenges of being well-endowed and showing that having a big penis isn't always as fun as people think.

CHAPTER TWENTY-ONE

The producer made it clear that the show would involve full-frontal nudity on national television. They wanted to feature a few 'gifted' guys with different perspectives, and my angle was that I was using my size to make money on OnlyFans. I knew this show would be a big deal, a groundbreaking look at a sensitive topic.

I was aware the show could out me to my wider family. My aunts and siblings knew I worked in porn and often that was gay porn, but they didn't know the specifics. This show would reveal those details, potentially causing problems even within my family. However, I knew the publicity from the show would boost my career, so after weighing everything up, I agreed to do it.

Filming was fun. I went all-in, doing whatever the producer wanted. They filmed me naked, with my cock on full display, getting undressed in a gym locker room. My main scene was a threesome with other OnlyFans creators, a couple called Bonnie and Tommy. The production team had hired a lovely apartment and that was where Bonnie, Tommy and I first met. They filmed us discussing and agreeing to how the sex scene would play out. We got each other's consent, and then the crew left us alone to film. They were just on the other side of the door, microphones picking up every grunt and squeal. When we finished, I walked out naked, feeling like a boss, grinned at the producer, and said, "Job done". It was wild. I couldn't believe they'd actually air it.

The director loved my willingness to just do whatever was required. However, they asked me to do something which shocked even me: measure my erect penis on camera. I just couldn't believe this would be shown on television, but I agreed without hesitation.

Arriving at the studio, a massive warehouse in London, I pushed open these large wooden doors and I stepped into this huge space which was empty other than a long boardroom table. Around this table sat the entire production team, a group of about 20 people, all staring at me with a mix of curiosity and amusement.

The crew had already seen what we had recorded so far, all seen me naked, all heard me making out with Bonnie and Tommy. Many of them had a kind of knowing look on their faces, others were openly grinning. One guy broke the ice and said, "Don't worry, Andy, we put the heating on for you upstairs so you don't have to 'perform' in the cold."

They had created a bedroom set upstairs, complete with professional lighting and cameras. I even had a teleprompter with a script on it. The director's instructions were clear: read the lines, get hard, and measure. The pressure was immense and I was wracked with nerves. The crew would leave

CHAPTER TWENTY-ONE

me in private, hiding round the corner as I watched a bit of porn on my phone to try and help get 'little Andy' fully erect. As soon as I did, I had to say the lines and measure. Then the whole crew of about 15 people would rush back in and reset everything for a different angle. As this was going on, I'd just be sitting there, going soft as lighting is moved and the make-up person is patting powder on my shiny face. Then they would leave me in private again and I'd have to try and get hard and do it all over again. This happened five times as they kept on wanting different angles!

Despite the challenges, the shoot was a success. I got over my nerves, 'little Andy' did me proud and I delivered a performance that pleased everyone!

A week before the show, the producer dropped a bombshell: they'd changed the title from "Too Large For Love" to "My Massive Cock"! I couldn't believe my eyes when I first saw it in print, with only a few asterisks to censor it: "My Massive C**k".

The night of the broadcast was a nerve-wracking thrill. I warned my family to brace themselves.

The show was well-made and informative. Other guys struggled with their size. One guy's penis was so large that it was always visible, no matter what he wore. Whether it was shorts, a suit, or sweatpants, it always looked like he had an erection. He was constantly stared at. Another guy, a footballer, had a massive cock that his teammates secretly filmed in the locker room showers and shared on WhatsApp. He'd go on dates with girls who'd already seen photos of his "trouser snake".

But I had a different story. I loved my big dick, and it was making me good money. The whole nation was talking about it. People who missed the live broadcast flocked to the streaming service to catch up. It went as far as Australia. The show was a huge hit, dominating the news and boosting my OnlyFans, with people keen to see the threesome that was filmed behind closed doors. It was a massive success.

The show's popularity, however, had a dark side. Some cruel individuals in Ireland discovered my brothers' previous adult work and began sharing explicit screenshots. They even sent these images to my aunts and sister, causing immense distress. One of my brothers was particularly affected and blamed me for the negative attention. As a result, we stopped communicating. I understand why he was upset; my newfound fame put a spotlight on his work, leading to unwanted backlash. I sincerely regret the pain he endured.

A few months later, my youngest brother, Ryan, the only one of us who hadn't done adult work, wanted to join the family business. I was against it, fearing the same backlash his brothers had faced. I reminded him how they'd struggled, and I didn't

CHAPTER TWENTY-ONE

want him to go through that. But Ryan thought it was unfair. He argued that if his brothers could do it, why couldn't he?

I talked to Aunt Teresa. She'd raised Ryan as though he was her own son after our mum passed away. In fact, Ryan called her Mum. She understood Ryan's stubbornness and agreed that if he was determined to do it, I should help him do it properly. We made a deal: he'd start his own OnlyFans page, and I'd guide him. He'd be a content creator in his own right, earning his own money. I'd share my expertise and help him navigate the industry.

Ryan thrived, and I'm proud of what he's accomplished. A leading Irish newspaper picked up the story and ran it with the headline 'OnlyFams', which we found hilarious. Of course, the online trolls had a field day, attacking Ryan, but he took it all in his stride. He takes after his big brother by not giving a single fuck what anyone thinks of him. Helping Ryan inspired me to create the world's first Porn Star University.

***

Chapter Twenty-Two

"PSU"

—

Once I started succeeding on OnlyFans, I frequently found myself being approached by other people, mainly guys, seeking advice on how to establish themselves as content creators. I realised that many people had unrealistic expectations, believing they could quickly become wealthy by simply posting a few videos of their feet on OnlyFans. It's really not that simple.

Dear readers,

Let me briefly interrupt this story to explain OnlyFans, as I've realised I've been assuming everyone knows how it works.

OnlyFans is primarily an adult content platform where individuals, known as creators, can offer exclusive content to subscribers by creating their own page. Creators can choose between two models: a monthly subscription, providing access to all content,

CHAPTER TWENTY-TWO

or a pay-per-view model, where subscribers purchase specific items.

I've opted for a subscription model, charging a monthly fee for access to my entire library of content, which I constantly update. OnlyFans shares revenue with creators, with an 80/20 split in favour of the creator.

OnlyFans prioritises privacy, as content isn't publicly visible. Potential viewers must create an account and subscribe to a creator's page to access their content. This means creators often rely on social media to promote their OnlyFans profiles and attract new subscribers.

Helping my brother Ryan establish his own OnlyFans page gave me a unique perspective on the challenges faced by newcomers to the industry. I realised that others were eager for similar guidance from me. Time and time again, I could see people trying and failing to launch their adult movie careers, and I could identify their mistakes. This inspired me to create the world's first Porn Star University (PSU).

Whenever anyone asks me about making adult content for OnlyFans, the first thing I say to them is, 'Could you cope if all your friends, family members, or potential future employers viewed your explicit content?' If they answer 'no', then I make it clear that this work isn't suitable. You see, as much as OnlyFans takes privacy seriously, it's just not possible to guarantee that footage won't be leaked and shared. Once it's on the internet, or shared via messaging apps, it's nearly impossible to stop that and make it disappear. I, of course, learnt this the hard way when I lost my job as a gas engineer.

I also like to really emphasise that if your motivation for doing this is to spice up your own sex life, then you're doing it for the wrong reasons. If you prioritise having and enjoying casual sexual encounters over building your business and making money, then you'll never be successful.

Only once I'm satisfied that they've properly considered all of the above and still want to proceed, will I invite them to train at PSU with the aim of joining 'Team Andy'.

The first thing I do with new lads at PSU is to establish the basics. This includes setting up their OnlyFans and social media accounts, as well as taking high-quality images and videos. I teach them the importance of having their paperwork in order. Mainly having model release forms, and appropriate ID of everyone they work with, which proves they have given consent and are of legal age.

To ensure they're properly focused, I also ask them to seriously consider what exactly they're selling, such as do they have a particular niche or kink. It's important to think of this as a business from the outset. If you don't know what you're selling,

CHAPTER TWENTY-TWO

you won't be able to find your audience. Knowing your audience and providing them with exactly what they want is the only way to be truly successful. My subscribers mean everything to me. I truly appreciate every single one of them and realise that without their support, I wouldn't be where I am now. So, I drum into everyone I train to treat their audience with respect and never take them for granted.

I've built a community of creators, connected through a WhatsApp group that I created, where we provide daily help and support. I'm passionate about the mental health of the creators in my community, and I encourage the guys to open up if they're feeling low, creating a safe space to share their experiences, both work-related and personal.

With OnlyFans, content is king, and most creators collaborate to create new content. My studio is the perfect place for this. Sometimes a few guys meet up, while other times it's a full-blown 'content day', which could involve up to 50 people.

I aim to make these days as productive as possible, going out of my way to ensure the lads have everything they need. I start by arriving early to turn on the heating and set up any necessary film sets, like a gym locker room or army barracks. I then go shopping for props, clothing, and plenty of food and drink to keep everyone fuelled.

SMELLY KID

These days are chaotic but fun. There's always something happening, from welcoming new creators to teaching them about lighting, camera angles, and other essential skills. Even if a new creator isn't quite ready to film adult content, they can still learn from watching the more experienced guys and from my guidance. It's a great way for them to gain confidence and learn the ropes.

The lads create crazy social media content to gain attention and promote their accounts, as well as filming raunchy material for OnlyFans. We've even revived the classic 'oil wrestling'!

Organising these days can be quite costly, especially feeding 50 hungry lads. But I don't charge the guys anything for my time or the resources I provide. I genuinely enjoy helping them succeed. One particularly rewarding experience was helping a man, Rich, who had recently been released from prison. He had nothing; but with my guidance, he now has a home, a car, and has reconnected with his son. Seeing guys like him thrive is the ultimate reward.

PSU became so famous it was even featured on a TV show. I was approached by a producer who was making a programme exploring how working in porn can negatively affect your life. They wanted to focus on my own experience of losing my job due to my employer's disgust at my past adult work.

CHAPTER TWENTY-TWO

However, rather than solely focusing on the negative impact, they also wanted to showcase how I'd turned the experience into a positive and was now thriving thanks to OnlyFans. A significant part of the show highlighted my work supporting up-and-coming creators through my PSU.

Amidst all this positivity I also decided to make a change to the content I produced. You see the airing of 'My Massive C**k' proved to be a liberating experience. With my quirky career choice now exposed to those closest to me, I felt a new sense of freedom to do whatever I wanted.

When my work as a porn star was revealed on national television, some friends and family members back in Dublin were disgusted with me and chose to cut me off completely.

While this was initially upsetting, I soon realised it was a useful cleansing process. It allowed me to appreciate the genuine support of those who stood by me, regardless of my profession. So yes, my friendship group might have shrunk, but those who remained mean the world to me. I felt incredibly fortunate to have such loving and understanding people in my life, and I still do.

It was this new sense of freedom that prompted the decision to push my boundaries further in my adult work. I began receiving oral sex from other men. This was something my fans had been requesting for years, but I had always hesitated.

Receiving oral sex from a dude isn't something I'd ever choose to do in private. I'm sexually attracted to women. However, I could see that my fans were craving more sexually explicit content than just solo masturbation. I realised that offering something more would be a significant boost to my business. It wasn't just my fans who had been asking me to do this. For over a decade, I'd been made multiple offers from porn directors to do this, but I'd always declined. There was no way I was going to allow them to profit from something that wasn't naturally easy for me to do.

But with OnlyFans, I had full control. I decided to push my boundaries. The movie showing me doing this for the first time was initially sold as pay-per-view. My fans went crazy for it, and it took my earnings to a whole new level, far beyond the dreams of the Andy who once moved rubble for £5 an hour.

***

Chapter Twenty-Three

"I'M OK"

—

Hello, dear reader! Well, that was quite a journey, wasn't it?

My story is nearly over, and as I write this in 2024, with a belly full of food, sitting in a beachside restaurant, I'm aware of just how far I've come from being the smelly kid I described in the opening chapters. I'm not mentioning the cooked meal or the Miami restaurant to boast. I hope I'm not that kind of person. However, I figured that if you've made it this far, you deserve to know that I'm doing well now, and I think you'll be interested to hear about what it's like for me no longer being poor.

Money doesn't necessarily bring happiness. I've lived for most of my life with barely any money and still managed to maintain a positive outlook. Even during my darkest moments, when I was lonely, scared, freezing, and hungry, sleeping in the back of my friend's car, I got through it by focusing on the fact that morning would eventually come, my friends would arrive, and new adventures would begin. I truly believe in the law of attraction. If I'd spent those nights focusing on how cold and hungry I was, I would have likely woken up feeling sad and sorry for myself. But I rarely did.

I'm actually lucky to have been fairly upbeat throughout most of my life. Even during the darkest periods, I usually found something positive to cling onto.

If I could offer one piece of advice, it would be this: no matter how terrible life gets, find one good thing to focus on. Doing so will usually lead to things becoming better, quicker than it would by solely concentrating on the negativity.

So, back to Miami! OnlyFans has changed my life in ways I could only have dreamed of, and yes, that's mainly due to the income it brings me.

I love to travel and have had so much fun exploring other countries and cultures. This year alone, I've travelled to Japan, India, Sri Lanka, Dubai, Spain, Romania, and the United States. I tend to spend a few weeks working hard at my studio, creating content, followed by several weeks of travel.

I mostly travel economy class, as I'm lucky enough to either fall asleep for most of the flight or lose myself in back-to-back movies. However,

CHAPTER TWENTY-THREE

occasionally, I'll treat myself to business class. Once, I even splurged on first class just to experience it. Wow!

Arriving at the airport, I had my own security channel and breezed through without any queues. I was able to relax in the British Airways Concorde Lounge, where they served fine wines with amazing food. Not that I drank any wine but even I could tell it was posh. Craig David was even sitting in the lounge nearby, and I was starstruck! A chauffeured car took me to the plane, where I was welcomed aboard and shown to my seat, 1K. The service was impeccable, and I felt truly special. Even now, I still struggle to believe that people don't view me as inferior. The British Airways crew were incredible, especially the flight attendant who looked after me through the flight. She laid out a tablecloth and a bewildering array of cutlery. I had to ask for help, and she kindly explained each utensil's purpose. Who knew there were special knives just for fish?

One habit I'm still trying to break is my tendency to sit at the table with my left arm wrapped around my plate, clutching my fork like a weapon. This habit stems from my childhood, when I had to protect my limited food supply from my mother's boyfriends and my siblings. It was a fight for survival! It's also probably no surprise to hear that I tend to wolf down my food at breakneck speed. Again, it's a habit I'm working on.

If I stay with friends, I'll often end up going to the shops intending to get an energy drink or similar and returning with a bag full of milk, bread, cheese, and jam for their fridge, whether they need it or not! Again, this likely stems from my desire to never be hungry again! My friends seem to find it cute.

In 2023, I was nominated for Male Performer of the Year by the SNAP Awards. Even being nominated was an incredible honour. Being recognised by the adult industry, especially by SNAP, was incredibly important to me. SNAP, headed by Mark Hassell, stands for Support Network for Adult Performers, providing invaluable services in areas such as sexual and mental health, data protection, and other critical topics relating to the adult business.

Honestly, I've never felt fully accepted by the industry I work in. The gay-for-pay niche is often looked down upon, and the big studios tend to distance themselves from it. Straight male performers who have worked in gay porn are also often shunned by these studios and I'm no exception. There's definitely a form of prejudice at play. It used to bother me, but now that I'm so busy and successful with my own work, I simply don't care.

I was up against huge industry stars who worked for the biggest studios, and I felt like I had no chance of winning. I put on my smartest clothes and turned up to the awards night mainly to show gratitude to

CHAPTER TWENTY-THREE

Mark for even knowing who I was. But I only went and bloody well won! Standing on that stage, holding that award in my hand brought a whirlwind of emotions to the surface. For a split second, I felt like an imposter, but I didn't allow myself to dwell on those feelings of unworthiness. I've worked incredibly hard to achieve what I have. Those who call me "lucky" have no idea about my journey. It wasn't luck that paid for my dream motorbike; it was getting my bare arse whipped with stinging nettles in a freezing forest. It wasn't 'luck' that got my work promoted in national newspapers for my antics in Paris and you'll forgive me for saying so, it wasn't 'luck' that put me in a position where I didn't have to worry what my parents thought about my career choice. I work hard, really hard. I spend countless hours each day promoting myself and creating content on social media. Organising content days at my studio takes a lot of time and effort. I know the sacrifices I've made, including being shunned by some family and friends, to achieve success in my work. So, I stood on that stage and accepted my award with immense pride because I truly deserved it.

This year, I got nominated again and I won for the second year running.

Early in 2023, I was approached by a documentary maker who wanted to produce a show about my life. The original idea was that it would tell the story I'm telling you now. However, once production started, it ended up taking a different direction, meaning you, dear reader, are the first people to hear the true story of where I came from.

As part of filming the documentary, now called 'OnlyAndy', I ended up returning to Dublin for the first time since I'd left. Landing at Dublin Airport brought up so many unexpected emotions, flashbacks of my terrible childhood that affected me so much, that when I stepped onto Irish soil, I was physically sick. I honestly just wanted to turn around and leave. However, I had work to do, so I put on a brave face and got on with it.

I returned to Dorset Street Flats, which were now empty and ready for demolition. Most of the buildings had already been flattened, but my old block still remained. Memories of Mum flooded back, mostly good ones. My time there was mainly happy, but those warm thoughts were tainted by the terrifying memory of being physically dragged from the flats by an angry, shouting mob.

I got the footage I needed and I couldn't leave Dublin fast enough.

We finished 'OnlyAndy' and it's now available to watch in many countries on Amazon. It focuses more on my work as a porn star and features lots of behind-the-scenes action.

When I started writing this book, I couldn't stop thinking about Teacher Brian and how kind he had

CHAPTER TWENTY-THREE

been to me. I hadn't heard of him since my Mum's funeral and wasn't sure if he was even still alive. Well, he is! It took a while to track him down, and when I first reached out, I wasn't even sure if I'd found the right person or if he'd remember me, let alone reply.

But, he did reply, and his response knocked me for six. He actually sent me voice notes, and listening to them brought tears to my eyes. I've never doubted my own story; I can remember so many details of my childhood as clearly as if they happened yesterday. However, I've also had to endure a lifetime of some family members telling me that it wasn't that bad. It felt like gaslighting. I lived through it, I know what happened. I suspect they want to downplay the situation to protect Mum's memory and to conceal their own guilt for not doing more to protect Mum and us kids. The same uncles and men who now shun me because of my work in gay porn are the same so-called men who did nothing when Mum was being beaten black and blue by John, or when I was sleeping rough as a teenager. If I sound bitter, I'm not. They made their choices, and I made mine. Their opinion of me is irrelevant to my life now.

Brian validated everything I knew to be true about how tough my younger life was in his voice messages. In fact, it was as if he'd already read this story.

SMELLY KID

Even though this is my book, and my story told in my words, it's been a team effort with my good friend Dave helping me piece it all together. He knows me better than most and has managed to get me to open up in ways I wasn't expecting when I started the writing process. I thought it would be a good idea to take Dave to Dublin so he could see some of the places I was talking about.

So, I made another journey to Ireland, and this time, it was less daunting having company. We visited so many places. The Regina Coeli Hostel is still there, its harsh brick exterior and tall wooden doors giving it an almost prison-like feel. I could see how it used to be a workhouse and even as an adult, I felt uneasy standing outside. I showed Dave some of the schools I attended and the long daily walks I took each day. He couldn't believe the distance. I was shocked too, but as a kid, you don't know any different. We caught up with my aunts, Teresa and Linda. They both seemed well and happy and shared memories of Mum. Linda actually lives just a few feet from the house I was living in when Mum died. As I looked at the front door, I had a flashback to pedalling away with John and having Patrick sitting on the crossbar. I walked along the street to the spot where I had my last hug from Mum. Then, Dave and I went and said hi to her as we visited the cemetery where she rests.

CHAPTER TWENTY-THREE

We also met TinTin. This time, I treated him to dinner and we had a delicious Chinese meal. TinTin is happy and thriving as a dad and I'm so proud of him.

However, the most emotional moment was my return to Sunshine House. It was exactly as I remembered. I could see they still had some of the same swings and roundabouts I played on as a kid. I walked down to the beach where we built sandcastles and remembered how we'd all run around completely carefree.

As I stood there outside Sunshine House, I was instantly transported back in time to a place where I felt safe, calm, happy, and even loved. I want to end this book by reassuring you, dear reader, that this is how I'm feeling in my life right now. It's been quite a journey to get here, and I thank you for travelling with me and allowing me to share it all with you. I'm Andy Lee and that was my story... for now.

✲✲✲

Message from Brian

Hi, Andrew. Brian O'Toole here, I can't believe you found me. You're amazing, and I'm looking at the picture of you. Oh, I can really see you. I can see you when you are very small.

This is unbelievable. I can't believe this. Firstly, I couldn't reply for about ten minutes. I was all kind of choked up. I still am, kind of, a bit because it's so good to hear your voice, and more than any of that, I'm just so glad that you're happy, and I'm really delighted that you're finding somebody who can help you unravel some of the stuff that you had that other children didn't have growing up.

There's an awful lot I can tell you about, really. Going right back to how it all kind of unravelled for your mum and the children at home, and how I found you one evening in winter huddled around one ring in a cooker and your mum had nothing.

MESSAGE FROM BRIAN

All the trips to Sunshine House for you and for your family, God, they were just super.

To the day I cut your hair. When I went down, I saw your mum cutting your hair. She was cutting the hair of yourself and Patrick. She actually had the two of you sitting on the fridge, and she was cutting the hair, and I saw what she was doing, and she kind of looked at me, and she saw my face, and she said, "Am I not doing it right?" And I couldn't say it. I just said, "Well, do you know?" I said. "There is a knack to it. I'm not very good at it, but I'll have a go." So she just handed me the scissors and off I went. I didn't do too bad a job. And she kind of said, "Actually, I'd have done it differently, and I'd have made a mess of it."

But she was lovely. Your mum was really lovely.

I mean, she was lovely.

She didn't have things easy.

She was different from other mums. But I can tell you for a fact that she loved all of you with her whole heart.

SMELLY KID

Yeah, there is a lot I can tell you.

I ended up going to court at one stage. When things happened, when your mum died, and there was, there was a question over who's going to mind you afterwards? And then there was the whole issue of who is John? And, oh, my God. It was heartbreaking. It was just hard. Even thinking back on it now reminds me so much. And if I'm not mistaken, some people went out of their way to tell you that John was not your dad. If I'm not mistaken, there was something about that I can't remember, but it just got very difficult.

Like, what was a really difficult time for you became even more difficult. And the only thing we could think of doing was to go to Sunshine twice a year, at least. That's a break. It's a holiday. And I used to just bring it myself, and I just round up you children, round up your brothers and sister, and I got into trouble all over the place. People said, "Oh, you're bringing the children down again." But I had a friend down there. I don't know if you remember her. She'd frighten the shit out of anybody, but she loved your family. So I always used to go down and I would say, "Can I bring them down?" And I'd

MESSAGE FROM BRIAN

bring them down on her week, because I knew she knew your story and thought of all of the children in Dublin at the moment, these children are amongst the most in need, so we have to do the most that we can for these children. And to be honest, Andrew, you were actually children who were in real need for a long time, and you really did have a difficult time, all of you.

There is an awful lot I can tell you about what happened going back to the time when one day you didn't turn up in school, and the neighbour had said, "We've put your family out of the Dorset Street flats." And I just heard this as I was passing in the door, and I said, "Sorry, what did you say there?" And she said, "Yes. They were kind of like a vigilante group, and they put your mum and the babies out." And when I went round to Dorset Street flats, they were putting your stuff out of the flat, the first thing I saw was a pram. And I thought, "Are you fucking telling me that you've put this mum out with four children and no pram?" And then it was a question of, "Where have they gone?" And nobody knew, and nobody cared. And it was, it was November. It was bloody November. I searched for about three or four days, and one night I ended up in this

SMELLY KID

place, in Church Street, and it was really dark. I found school jumpers on a clothesline, soaking wet in the lashing rain, and I knew then that you were here somewhere. So I knocked on every door, and I found you.

And then the first thing I got was a pram, and I said to your mum, "The boys are going back to school tomorrow. Because if they come back to school, then you have room to figure out where you're going to live and what you're going to do." And for a little while, you went into a place called Regina Coeli Hostel and you had your first Christmas there, and we did Santa and got toys. We made sure everything could be as good as it was.

And then you went to the cottages in Croke Villas. And you were there for a little while, and after that, then it was your mum's accident, and the fright that was for everybody, oh, my God. And then I got to meet your grandparents and John. And that brought in a whole lot more issues and trouble.

And it was at that stage then, because people knew I knew the family quite well, and even though I wasn't your teacher, I kept in touch

MESSAGE FROM BRIAN

with you the whole way and we were going up and down to Sunshine, people said the only person who knows that family reasonably well is Brian O'Toole. So that's how come social workers came to me and said, "Listen, can you help us out here?" So I filled in as much as I could, and that's how I ended up going to court. And I met some of your other family through the court, but anyway, and at that stage, then others were looking after you, I think there were uncles and aunts, and because you moved away, I never really saw you again. But there we go. Anyway. This has turned out to be very long.

But look, these are just some of the things. So all I'm saying to you is, have a think about some of the questions. Come back and ask, and then when we meet, I can fill in lots more.

It was really, really lovely to hear from you. I mean, I don't know how many times I've thought about you and all your family, and still do even at Christmas time. And I have the most beautiful photo of you when you were small, taken in school. I think you were four or five, and I remember printing it out for your mum, and she was delighted with it. And I printed out a couple of copies, I think. But anyway, I've kept one. I'll find it. I have it somewhere. I kept one. It's a beautiful photo, and I'll send you a copy of it.

***

Acknowledgments

I want to begin by thanking my incredible mum, *Louise,* who brought me into this world. She gave me life and did everything in her power to make sure I was loved and cared for, despite the many obstacles life threw her way. *Mum, you were my best friend, my absolute everything. When you were taken away from me, I lost all hope. Over time, I thought back to all those conversations we had when you told me, no matter how hard life is, to focus on the good things. For you, those good things were me, my brothers, and my sister. You also told me to stay in school to be a doctor one day. Well, I've been a doctor, firefighter, police officer, and many more haha. I wish you could see the man I've become today. I carry your fight in my soul and your love in my heart. I am everything I am today because of you. Thank you, Mum.*

To my siblings, *Patrick, Aoife, Dan, Connor,* and *Ryan*: After everything we've been through together. Despite all the challenges we faced, we are still standing strong against the world with Mum looking down on us.

I would also like to extend my heartfelt thanks to *Brian O'Toole*. Not only was he my primary school teacher, but he became the caring male figure in my life at a time when I needed it most. Brian was there for me when no one else was. He went above and beyond for me and my family when he didn't have to, and he never judged us when others did. He stood by me when my mum passed away, and for that, I will always be grateful.

To my friend *Dave*: Thank you for your constant guidance in my adult life and for helping me write this book. You helped me dig deep into my past, uncovering my darkest memories and experiences that I had locked away. You have been a great support and friend throughout my journey.

To *Clayton*: From the moment we met, you saw me in need, and without hesitation, you opened your heart and home. You became my best friend and brother. You always put others first. *Clayton, bro, I miss you every single day. I hope you're jamming up there to all our favourite songs. The day I left Ireland at the airport, you told me to go, live my life, and not look back. I can honestly tell you, bro, I'm living my life to the max, and I have your tattoo on my arm, with me every step of the way.*

ACKNOWLEDGMENTS

To *Tintin*: You gave me friendship and love when everyone else turned their back on me. You saw me at my lowest and stayed by my side when I reached my peak. You have so little, but you would give the world to anyone who needed it. Thank you, bro.

To *OnlyFans*: Thank you for giving me a second chance at life and the opportunity to connect with my fans on a personal level. You gave me the space to express myself through content that I control, and for that, I will always be grateful.

To *my fans*: I would like to take a moment to thank each and every one of you who has supported me throughout my journey. Your encouragement and love mean the world to me. I am so grateful for our daily conversations. From the guy who once felt invisible, you all have made me feel on top of the world. Thank you.

Finally, to *everyone* who has been part of my journey, and to *the universe* that continues to unfold before me, remember: *Live your life to the fullest. Today, you can have something, and tomorrow it could be gone. Share love and positivity with everyone around you. Life is what you make of it. My journey continues, and I'm excited for what lies ahead.*